THE 24:7 DAD

THE 24/7 DAD

THE 24:7 DAD

12 Habits of Confident Fathers

CHRISTOPHER A. BROWN

JOSSEY-BASS
A Wiley Brand

Copyright © 2026 by Christopher A. Brown. All rights reserved.

Published by John Wiley & Sons, Inc., Hoboken, New Jersey.

No part of this publication may be reproduced, stored in a retrieval system, or transmitted in any form or by any means, electronic, mechanical, photocopying, recording, scanning, or otherwise, except as permitted under Section 107 or 108 of the 1976 United States Copyright Act, without either the prior written permission of the Publisher, or authorization through payment of the appropriate per-copy fee to the Copyright Clearance Center, Inc., 222 Rosewood Drive, Danvers, MA 01923, (978) 750-8400, fax (978) 750-4470, or on the web at www.copyright.com. Requests to the Publisher for permission should be addressed to the Permissions Department, John Wiley & Sons, Inc., 111 River Street, Hoboken, NJ 07030, (201) 748-6011, fax (201) 748-6008, or online at http://www.wiley.com/go/permission.

The manufacturer's authorized representative according to the EU General Product Safety Regulation is Wiley-VCH GmbH, Boschstr. 12, 69469 Weinheim, Germany, e-mail: Product_Safety@wiley.com.

Trademarks: Wiley and the Wiley logo are trademarks or registered trademarks of John Wiley & Sons, Inc. and/or its affiliates in the United States and other countries and may not be used without written permission. All other trademarks are the property of their respective owners. John Wiley & Sons, Inc. is not associated with any product or vendor mentioned in this book.

Limit of Liability/Disclaimer of Warranty: While the publisher and the author have used their best efforts in preparing this work, including a review of the content of the work, neither the publisher nor the author make any representations or warranties with respect to the accuracy or completeness of the contents of this work and specifically disclaim all warranties, including without limitation any implied warranties of merchantability or fitness for a particular purpose. Certain AI systems have been used in the creation of this work. No warranty may be created or extended by sales representatives, written sales materials or promotional statements for this work. The fact that an organization, website, or product is referred to in this work as a citation and/or potential source of further information does not mean that the publisher and author endorse the information or services the organization, website, or product may provide or recommendations it may make. This work is sold with the understanding that the publisher is not engaged in rendering professional services. The advice and strategies contained herein may not be suitable for your situation. You should consult with a specialist where appropriate. Further, readers should be aware that websites listed in this work may have changed or disappeared between when this work was written and when it is read. Neither the publisher nor author shall be liable for any loss of profit or any other commercial damages, including but not limited to special, incidental, consequential, or other damages.

For general information on our other products and services or for technical support, please contact our Customer Care Department within the United States at (800) 762-2974, outside the United States at (317) 572-3993 or fax (317) 572-4002.

Wiley also publishes its books in a variety of electronic formats. Some content that appears in print may not be available in electronic formats. For more information about Wiley products, visit our web site at www.wiley.com.

Library of Congress Cataloging-in-Publication Data

Names: Brown, Christopher A. (Executive), author.
Title: The 24:7 dad : 12 habits of confident fathers / Christopher A. Brown.
Description: [San Francisco, California] : Jossey-Bass, [2026]
Identifiers: LCCN 2026006432 (print) | LCCN 2026006433 (ebook) | ISBN 9781394382354 (paperback) | ISBN 9781394382378 (adobe pdf) | ISBN 9781394382361 (epub)
Subjects: LCSH: Fatherhood. | Parenting. | Child rearing.
Classification: LCC HQ756 .B785 2026 (print) | LCC HQ756 (ebook)
LC record available at https://lccn.loc.gov/2026006432
LC ebook record available at https://lccn.loc.gov/2026006433

Cover Design: Jon Boylan
Author photo by Kayla Cates
SKY10151490_040126

*To my daughters, Alexis Christine and Jillian Rose,
and my wife and co-parent, Kayla.*

Contents

Preface: Boys, Balls, and Backyards		*xi*
Introduction		*xvii*
1	**The 6 Traits & 12 Habits of the 24:7 Dad**	1
2	**Self-Awareness: Accountability & Reflection**	15
3	**Self-Care: Physical & Mental Health**	33
4	**Fathering Skills: Holistic Fathering & Modeling Healthy Masculinity**	67
5	**Parenting Skills: Nurturing & Disciplining Your Children**	99
6	**Relationship Skills: Communicating Effectively & Co-Parenting Relationships**	137
7	**Stewardship: Paying It Forward and Engaging Your Community**	175
8	**Stepping Out of Your Comfort Zone**	199
	Appendix: The Value in Married Fatherhood	*207*
	Acknowledgments	*217*
	About the Author	*219*
	Index	*221*

Preface
Boys, Balls, and Backyards

> *"Boys want to grow up to be like their male role models. And boys who grow up in homes with absent fathers search the hardest to figure out what it means to be male."*
> —Geoffrey Canada, founder and president of Harlem Children's Zone

The day my first child was born, I felt completely lost and overwhelmed knowing this seven-pound life depended on me for survival, guidance, love, and strength. Growing up without an involved father, I had no idea how to be the father she needed me to be.

My First Model of a Father

Growing up, life around the dinner table formed my first model of a father—I learned that he wasn't involved in his children's lives. My father was a university professor and department head. His workaholic tendencies meant he was rarely home (and if he made it home for dinner, he often went right back to work). The nights he was home weren't pretty. When my father got angry or disappointed with me or my brother, he would often yell and become verbally abusive, even over minor things like spilling milk on the table. He was extremely critical, cutting us to the bone with his intelligence, command of English, and deep, powerful voice. My mother called him a "rage-a-holic."

A Baseball, Two Mitts, and a Backyard

The most significant moment in my childhood occurred when I was 12. When you think about fathers spending time with their sons, a classic American image that comes to mind is playing catch. I tried to persuade my father to play catch with me for years, but he refused. I was shocked and excited when, one day, he agreed. I ran to my room, grabbed two mitts and a baseball, and met him in the backyard. I handed him a mitt and, unsure whether he could catch, directed him to stand just 10 yards away. I softly tossed the ball to him and was shocked a second time—he could catch! He could also throw, though not accurately.

After a few tosses back and forth, I directed him to stand another 10 yards away. I warned him to expect a harder throw. I hummed the ball toward him and the ball popped in his mitt. If you've played baseball, you know there's no better sound than a ball you've thrown popping a mitt, especially when the recipient drops their mitt and rubs their hand. Their typical reaction is one of respect—a nod of the head, a smile, or a return throw that pops your mitt. That wasn't my father's reaction. After dropping the mitt and ball, he moved toward me, angrily pointing his finger, yelling, "I knew this was a bad idea! I'll never do it again!" He stormed inside, slamming the door. My excitement turned to disappointment when I realized that my father would spend time with me only on his terms and around his interests. Our relationship grew more distant.

A Golf Ball, Clubs, and Another Backyard

During the same year as the baseball-catching moment with my father, I fell in love with golf. Introduced to the game by one of my best friends, I learned quickly. And for the next few years, I took lessons from the men's golf coach at the same university where my father taught.

He was an excellent coach. Relaxed, patient, and encouraging, he couldn't have contrasted more with my uptight, impatient, and volatile father. Coach often connected a golf lesson to a life lesson, such as linking the importance of focusing on my short game to the significance of paying attention to the details that make all the difference in executing any skill well. He became an important father figure to me.

Coach focused on the psychological aspect of the game—that which takes place between the ears separates great golfers as much as, or more than, their physical skills. I struggled with that part of the game. What I didn't realize at the time was how deeply my poor relationship with my father affected me. I was developing an anxious mindset that lacked the confidence necessary to succeed in any sport or professional endeavor. I would play brilliantly one round but terribly the next. I often got angry. Sometimes, I beat the ground with my club after a wayward shot. Sometimes, I threw clubs. I snapped a club or wrapped one around a tree a few times. I couldn't let go of the last shot or bad round and move on. I obsessed over what went wrong. (You'll learn about the role confidence plays in fathering in the Introduction.)

My Friends' Fathers

I had a handful of close friends at any given time. I enjoyed spending time with their families because they engaged in activities together that had nothing to do with work, and they truly enjoyed each other's company. What I noticed in those families was involved fathers. My friends were much closer to their fathers. Their fathers spent weekends sharing hobbies with their children, especially their sons, and they were curious about my interests and shared their own with me, like fishing and hunting.

Being exposed to men and fathers who treated me differently signaled that something was seriously wrong with my relationship with my father and where family fit into his priorities. I struggled to understand why my own father didn't support my interests, and I struggled to comprehend why I couldn't have the kind of relationship with him that my friends had with their fathers. I realized how fathers could wound their children even if, like my father, they didn't intend to. When my parents divorced during my senior year in high school, it had been a long time coming. I felt relieved and elated when he left.

Therapy, Fraternity, and Friendship

As I entered my teenage years, I began to wonder if something was wrong with me—something that caused my father to reject me. I was wounded. I struggled to process and share my feelings. I had anxiety that manifested in a series of obsessive habits, which were debilitating at times. My mother recognized that I needed the support of a trained professional to discuss and manage my intense feelings of hatred toward my father and the impact they had on me and my family.

My therapist was the second relaxed, patient, and encouraging adult male who became a father figure. He helped me separate from my father and appreciate and trust myself. He helped me realize there was nothing wrong with me and that I had the control to shape the kind of person I was and the father I could become.

The benefits of therapy, and the relief from not having to be around my father after the divorce, helped me to focus on my future.

I was shy in high school, but became more outgoing in college, joining a fraternity. I hoped it would provide the structured environment I needed to build a social life. It worked. I thrived in college and took on leadership roles in the fraternity and on campus. The fraternity connected me with other young men in a way that further aided my healing; their support and belief in me built my confidence.

In graduate school, I met a man who would change my life forever.

Jon wasn't a classmate; he was a volunteer facilitator in a 12-Step program modeled after Alcoholics Anonymous. Known as Co-Dependents Anonymous (CoDA), it helps people heal from the wounds of unhealthy relationships and build healthier ones.

Jon and I connected immediately. When he shared, it was clear that he had a father wound. After a few one-on-one talks following CoDA meetings, he invited me to join a group of men working to heal from their pain. It wasn't part of a larger movement or nationwide network, just a gathering of men focusing on mutual support and healing. We concentrated on helping one another become the best men we could be. The fathers in the group shared how their growth as men made them better fathers.

For the first time, I recognized the connection between being a good man and a good father, as well as the value of men's support groups. That's when I knew I wanted to help other men heal from the father wound, to fill that hole in their soul in the shape of their dad.

Introduction

"Confidence is a sense of certainty about your ability, which allows you to bypass conscious thought and execute unconsciously."

—Dr. Nate Zinnser, performance psychologist

Congratulations! In picking up this book, you've taken a vital step toward becoming the confident father you were meant to be. That step reflects intention. But intending to be a good father isn't enough. The world is littered with fathers who intended to be a good one, but who didn't act on their intention. You're not one of them. You're ready to act on your intention.

Who Is This Book For?

This book is for any man raising children. It's for biological, step, and adoptive fathers. It's also for "social fathers" or "father figures"—uncles, cousins, grandfathers, or any male stepping in to raise children who are disconnected from their fathers. Whether you're a married father living with your children, a divorced father living apart from them, a never-married father without custody, a single father raising your children, or any other kind of father, you're in the right place.

Building Your Fathering Confidence

What you do on your fathering journey has numerous benefits and will positively impact your family and future generations. No matter where you are on that journey, *The 24:7 Dad: 12 Habits of Confident Fathers* aims to help you become the confident father you were meant to be.

Fathering confidence—your level of belief in your ability to be a good father—is one of many factors that influence a father's involvement in his children's lives, including:

- Individual factors, such as your attitudes about the importance of your involvement, your children's ages, your ability to effectively co-parent, and your willingness to balance work and family life.

- Relational factors, such as the type and quality of the relationship with your children's co-parent, whether or not you live with your children, whether or not you have custody of them, and whether you live in a blended family.

- Cultural and systemic factors related to interactions with societal institutions like employers, corrections systems, child welfare, child support, and the courts.

I've spent my professional career monitoring research focused on understanding these factors. Fathering confidence has emerged as one of the most critical factors for all fathers. Confidence is a feeling that arises from knowledge and a specific skill set that you trust will work naturally whenever you call on it. It's like an emergency fund filled with deposits from all your positive fathering experiences—fathering wins. You'll draw from those wins when you must rely on your confidence to perform as a father, especially when you encounter new fathering challenges.[1] If you're not confident in your ability to care for and raise your children effectively, you'll always be behind the eight ball. We'll work together to build a rock-solid foundation of confidence in your fathering.

The knowledge and skills you'll gain from this book will help you open your fathering emergency fund. Your application of the 6 traits and 12 habits we'll discuss will act as automatic deposits into that fund. Those deposits are crucial for the persistence—the withdrawals—you'll need to solve fathering challenges.[2]

Fathering Winning Streaks

Building fathering confidence will reduce the uncertainty surrounding your ability to father effectively. As you build this confidence, it will create a self-reinforcing cycle: confidence breeds more confidence. This confidence will fuel more fathering wins. As in sports, you'll string wins together to form winning streaks.

In becoming a more confident father, you'll experience fathering losses. You're going to disappoint your children, your co-parent, and yourself. But as any baseball manager will tell you, it's more important to focus on winning two out of three games in a series rather than winning all three. String enough series wins together, and you'll likely make the playoffs. That's the kind of fathering winning streak you want.

The fathering confidence that winning streaks build will make you more resilient when the inevitable pain points arise. Continuity

---

[1] Zinsser, N. (2022). *The confident mind: A battle-tested guide to unshakable performance.* Mariner Books.
[2] Kanter, R. M. (2004). *Confidence: How winning streaks and losing streaks begin and end.* Crown Business.

breeds faith during adversity. Fathering winning streaks create the belief that you can bounce back from losses. As long as you stay disciplined in applying the 12 habits and remain humble, you can avoid losing streaks. Losing streaks are more likely when you convince yourself that you no longer need to apply the habits. Don't lose focus on the habits or you'll slowly drift away from them and wake up one day wondering why you're not the confident father you want to be.

Benefits of Involved Fathers

Becoming a 24:7 Dad begins with understanding why you and every other father are crucial to the well-being of children, families, and communities. Decades of research have shown that fathers play a crucial role in the well-being of children, families, and communities.[3] When I started working with National Fatherhood Initiative® (NFI), many Americans weren't convinced of this idea. They saw an involved father as a nice-to-have, not a necessity. While there's no longer a debate about the importance of fathers for child, family, and community well-being, we still have a lot of work ahead to ensure that as many children as possible have involved fathers. One challenge is that many Americans don't fully grasp why fathers are important because they're unaware of the myriad benefits that involved fathers provide.

First and foremost, involved fathers benefit children. The benefits start from the moment children are born and extend into adulthood. Children with involved fathers face a lower risk of infant mortality, low birth weight, emotional and behavioral issues, neglect and abuse, injuries, obesity, poor academic performance, teenage pregnancy, juvenile incarceration, alcohol and substance abuse, criminal behavior, and

---

[3]Brown, C., Trahan, M., Garnett-Deakin, A., Pond, E., Cho, S., & Gibson, S. (2024). *Father Facts™ 9*. National Fatherhood Initiative®.

suicide. When these children reach adulthood, they're more likely to have high-quality romantic relationships and less likely to commit domestic violence.

Mothers with engaged fathers in their children's lives also benefit in many ways. These mothers are more likely to receive prenatal care, less likely to smoke during pregnancy, and have healthier birth outcomes. They also face a lower risk of postpartum depression and stress, have reduced parenting stress, more leisure time, and higher-quality co-parenting relationships, and higher marital satisfaction.

And when fathers are involved in their children's lives, those men are happier, live longer, and are more active in their communities and civic groups. They have less depression and have more confidence and self-esteem. They're motivated to adopt a healthier model of masculinity, reduce alcohol and substance use, find stable jobs, better manage and save money, and strengthen family connections.

Today's Fathers

Becoming a 24:7 Dad involves understanding how the meaning of fatherhood has evolved in exciting ways. Today's fathers spend more time on the basic care and upbringing of their children. According to the U.S. Census Bureau, in the past two decades, the amount of time that married and cohabiting fathers spend caring for their children weekly has risen by 18 percent and 31 percent, respectively. Millennial fathers spend three times as much time per week caring for their children compared to fathers in the 1960s.[4]

One factor contributing to this evolution is the deeper role that being a father plays in men's lives. The Pew Research Center found

---

[4]Livingston, G., & Parker, K. (2019, June 12). *8 facts about American dads*. Pew Research Center. https://www.pewresearch.org/short-reads/2019/06/12/fathers-day-facts/

recently that 61 percent of dads consider being a father central to their personal identity.[5] They see providing for their family as much more important than succeeding at work.[6] Compared to previous generations, today's fathers embrace a more engaged and nurturing approach to fathering. According to the Survey of Contemporary Fatherhood, which included more than 2,100 fathers nationwide, today's fathers are more likely to be expressive and less likely to discipline their children harshly.[7]

Another contributing factor is fathers' willingness to acknowledge that raising children is hard and why it's hard. According to the Pew Research Center, most of today's fathers (58 percent) say parenting is much harder than they thought it would be.[8] One reason is they struggle more with work–family balance than previous generations. Studies also show that they report as much or more work–family conflict than mothers, particularly in dual-earner families.[9]

Because of these factors, today's fathers are more comfortable seeking help, particularly regarding child development, co-parenting,

---

[5]Schaeffer, K. (2023, June 15). *Key facts about dads in the U.S.* Pew Research Center. https://www.pewresearch.org/short-reads/2023/06/15/key-facts-about-dads-in-the-us/

[6]Global Strategy Group. (2025, June). *New poll results: Men feel strongly about family care and are making it a priority* [Memo]. https://globalstrategygroup.com/wp-content/uploads/2025/06/PLFA-Men-Survey-Memo-F06.02.25.pdf

[7]Thomas, C. R., & Holmes, E. K. (2020). Are father depression and masculinity associated with father perceptions of maternal gatekeeping? *Journal of Family Psychology, 34*(4), 490–495.

[8]Minkin, R., & Horowitz, J. M. (2023, January 24). *How U.S. mothers, fathers differ on parenting: Survey report (2023)*. Pew Research Center. https://www.pewresearch.org/social-trends/2023/01/24/gender-and-parenting/

[9]Brown, C., Trahan, M., Cho, S., Ezra, P., Garnett-Deakin, A., & Gibson, S. (2025). *Father Facts™ 9*. National Fatherhood Initiative.

child discipline, communication, work–family balance, and, increasingly, mental health. They seek solutions and tools to tackle the modern challenges of parenting. They're also more interested in connecting with other fathers for guidance and mutual support. You're not alone in turning to this book for support.

> **Children Without Fathers in Their Homes**
>
> *Imagine for a moment you're in New York City's Times Square. As you look around, you see only children, no adults. You walk down any street, board any subway train, enter any building, and still see only children.*
>
> *That eerie scene isn't as far from reality as you might think. Today, 18.2 million children in America (or 1 in 4) grow up without a biological, step, or adoptive father in their home.[10] That's enough children to populate New York City twice and Los Angeles four times!*
>
> *Children who grow up without a father in their home are at greater risk of poor physical, mental, and social outcomes. This doesn't mean that every child without a father in their home is doomed. Many children have involved fathers who don't live with them. However, the risks of negative outcomes are too steep to ignore.*

What to Expect in This Book

The following chapters serve as the flight plan for your journey to become a 24:7 Dad. As your co-pilot, I'll introduce you to the 6 traits and 12 habits that will help you become the confident father you want to be (and that your children need). Throughout the book, I'll share quick wins, motivating tips, and guidance you can apply immediately.

---

[10]U.S. Census Bureau. (2025). *Living arrangements of children under 18 years old: 1960 to present.* U.S. Census Bureau.

I'll give you activities to do that include answering questions, completing brief statements, and in-depth reflections (Deep Dives) to introduce the 12 habits and help you apply and customize them in ways that will have the maximum impact in your life. I'll also give you guidance and tips (Quick Wins) that you can use immediately to start applying the habits.

This learning method calls for your active participation—a strategy most books don't use but that's far more effective at helping you retain what you read. Participating in the activities requires writing—putting pen (or pencil) to paper—which activates your brain in a deeper way than passive reading. Writing enhances your ability to retain all the new knowledge and skills you'll learn because you have to pause, concentrate, and think critically about how to apply and customize the habits in ways that work for you.

I've been where you are in desiring to improve in an area of my life. I've picked up books that I hoped would be helpful. The best of those books required my active participation in learning. I read them with excitement, but most of the time what I learned didn't stick because I didn't do the activities, thinking they weren't important, and I didn't want to take the time to participate. It wasn't until I started actively participating in my learning that I started seeing the improvements I wanted.

I've also seen the power that this learning method has in transforming the lives of fathers who have participated in NFI programs. It helps fathers maximize the impact of what they learn. Without this approach, our programs wouldn't have teeth. The good news is many of the activities in this book are straight out of NFI programs and are proven to help fathers make change happen. *To facilitate your active participation, I created a worksheet that you can download from confidentfathers.com.* It's available as a Word document and PDF. Enter the URL into a search engine or scan the QR code at the end of this Introduction. Use it to complete the activities throughout the book.

In addition to being an active participant, I encourage you to focus on the following practices to get the most out of the 24:7 Dad traits and habits we'll be discussing:

- Acceptance of yourself (past and present) and others
- Gratitude for your strength and what you'll gain when you build the traits, apply the habits, and enlist the help of others
- Patience with yourself as you apply the habits and with others as they accept the changes these habits will bring
- Compassion for yourself when applying the habits—they require time—and consideration for how others might react to the changes
- Curiosity about applying habits and growing as a father, seeking new information and experiences that enhance your awareness, knowledge, and skills
- Trust in research-backed habits and faith that others care enough to help you instill them
- Focus on habits you can control rather than those requiring others to change their behavior

You'll also find hypothetical prompts that I created to illustrate how you can use artificial intelligence (AI) in applying and customizing the 12 habits and as an ongoing resource in your fathering journey. A few specific AI tools are ChatGPT, Claude, and Gemini. I've found them helpful in my professional and personal life, including my fathering.

Including these prompts isn't a statement that you must use AI tools to be a 24:7 Dad. While they can be helpful, there's a risk in using them. The information they provide (outputs) can be inaccurate. Additionally, an AI tool doesn't know anything about you or your life other than what you tell it. It might suggest things that aren't realistic for you to use. Take what you want from what an AI tool gives you and leave the rest.

A Few Notes on Language

I want to ensure we're on the same page about the meaning of a few words that I use throughout this book: fathering, co-parent, and co-parenting. I rarely use the word "fatherhood," which refers to a time in a man's life cycle. "Fathering," though, is the important work you do during that time. This book is for all types of fathers who are raising their children with another person, known as their "co-parent." "Co-parenting" refers to the efforts of two or more adults working together to care for and raise children they share responsibility for. It includes all family structures, no matter the parents' marital status or living situation. It focuses on how well parents cooperate in raising their children.

Given that most research on fathering, parenting, and co-parenting has involved fathers in heterosexual relationships—and since the vast majority of fathers are in such relationships—I'll sometimes refer to women (mothers) as co-parents when sharing details from research. That doesn't mean I'm overlooking fathers raising children with other co-parents. On the contrary, fathers raising children in any context will benefit from the guidance in this book.

A Pledge of Commitment

At the beginning of this Introduction, I called out your intention to be a 24:7 Dad and the importance of acting on that intention. To support your effort, I want you to create a short, motivational pledge. You can use the template below or make one from scratch.

> I commit to being a 24:7 Dad.
> I commit to being the father that [insert the names of your children] need me to be.

I commit to being the co-parent that
[insert the name of your co-parent] deserves.
I commit to giving everything I have to applying
the 12 habits of the 24:7 Dad.

Write down or type and print the pledge, then post it where you'll see it each day. Reciting the pledge daily will help you follow through on the long-term commitment to be a 24:7 Dad.

The pledge is a "commitment device" that involves making a public promise to yourself, your children, and your co-parent that you'll be the best father possible. Research shows that making a commitment known to others increases the likelihood that someone will follow through on behavior change.[11] To further solidify your commitment, make a copy for each of your children and your co-parent and sign them. Additionally, put the pledge on your social media profiles.

Confidentfathers.com

Scan the QR code below to access the worksheet and other supporting resources I'll point you to later in this book.

---

[11]Nudge, R. H., & Sunstein, C. R. (2021). *Nudge: The final edition*. Penguin Books.

Chapter 1

The 6 Traits & 12 Habits of the 24:7 Dad

"We are what we repeatedly do. Excellence, then, is not an act, but a habit."

—Aristotle, philosopher

Being a 24:7 Dad means that you're a confident father who knows how to be involved in his children's lives. It doesn't mean being physically present in your children's lives 24 hours a day, 7 days a week. That's impossible and, quite frankly, not healthy for you or your children. Being a 24:7 Dad means that you're striving to be the best father you can be around the clock, *based on your circumstances*. This book will assist you in *customizing your fathering* so that you can become the confident father your children need you to be.

The 6 Traits of the 24:7 Dad

Becoming a 24:7 Dad involves building the 6 traits of an involved and confident father. The traits are what separates the 24:7 Dad from uninvolved fathers who don't believe in their ability to be a good father. The traits encompass what the 24:7 Dad knows and how he acts:

1. **Self-awareness.** The 24:7 Dad is aware of who he is as a man and a father. He's aware of his importance to his family. He knows his moods, feelings, capabilities, strengths, and challenges.

He's responsible for his behavior and knows that his growth depends on how well he knows and accepts himself. He also knows that his ability to be with his children is affected by the choices he makes and accepts responsibility for those choices.

2. **Self-care.** The 24:7 Dad prioritizes his physical and mental health. He schedules annual check-ups, eats nutritious foods, exercises regularly, and seeks knowledge about the world around him. He understands the link between his physical and mental well-being. He fosters a strong bond with his family and community, surrounding himself with friends who encourage his healthy lifestyle. The 24:7 Dad is a model of self-worth through his healthy choices.

3. **Fathering skills.** The 24:7 Dad knows his role in the family. He knows he's a model for his children on how to be a good man and father. He knows that, when possible, he should be involved in the daily lives of his children—from getting them up, dressed, and fed in the mornings, to attending parent–teacher conferences, to supporting them in sports and other interests and activities, to helping them with their homework, to tucking them in at night. The 24:7 Dad applies his understanding of the unique skills he and his co-parent bring to raising their children.

4. **Parenting skills.** The 24:7 Dad nurtures his children. He knows how his parenting skills contribute to their physical, emotional, intellectual, social, spiritual, and creative development. His children trust him and feel safe because he cares for and nurtures them using proven parenting skills. The 24:7 Dad uses discipline and consequences to teach and guide his children, not to threaten or harm them.

5. **Relationship skills.** The 24:7 Dad builds and maintains healthy relationships with his children, co-parent, other family members, friends, and the community. He knows and values

how relationships shape his children. He knows how his relationship with his co-parent impacts his children and strives to create a positive relationship with them for their benefit. He seeks to enhance his communication skills.

6. **Stewardship.** The 24:7 Dad is thankful for what he has and learns. He knows that he's part of a community of fathers—a brotherhood committed to supporting other fathers. He doesn't keep his knowledge about being a good father to himself. He shares his insights with others, thereby contributing to the well-being of other fathers, children, and families in his community. He supports his community by participating in its civic life.

You'll build these traits through the application of the 12 habits we'll be discussing. Think about the 24:7 Dad as a house. The traits are the bricks that comprise the house. The habits are the mortar that we'll use to bind the bricks together. As you apply the mortar, the habits, the traits will build a more confident father over time. We'll discuss the knowledge, attitudes, and skills—the mortar's ingredients—that you'll need to apply the habits successfully.

The 12 Habits of the 24:7 Dad

As I mentioned in the Introduction, I've spent my career understanding the factors that motivate fathers to be involved in their children's lives and how confidence has emerged as one of the most critical factors. I've examined the research not only on what motivates fathers' involvement, but that provides evidence for what motivates individuals to engage in any behavior that benefits themselves and others. That approach allowed me to identify and integrate into National Fatherhood Initiative® (NFI) programs what works in areas like raising self-awareness and improving physical and mental health care to effective fathering.

Applying the right habits lies at the heart of effective, sustainable behaviors that benefit you and others. This is why the 12 habits matter in building the 6 traits and lead to confident fathering. There are two habits that help build each of the traits:

1. Working with an accountability partner (*self-awareness*)
2. Weekly reflection on your actions (*self-awareness*)
3. Regular physical care (*self-care*)
4. Regular mental health (*self-care*)
5. Holistic fathering (*fathering skills*)
6. Modeling healthy masculinity (*fathering skills*)
7. Nurturing your children (*parenting skills*)
8. Disciplining your children in healthy ways (*parenting skills*)
9. Communicating effectively (*relationship skills*)
10. Creating a loving co-parenting relationship (*relationship skills*)
11. Paying it forward (*stewardship*)
12. Engaging your community (*stewardship*)

You'll learn more in the following chapters exactly why these habits work. For now, I want you to understand that they work together. They're not a collection of separate habits operating in isolation. The model below reveals that they're part of a system. They reinforce one another.

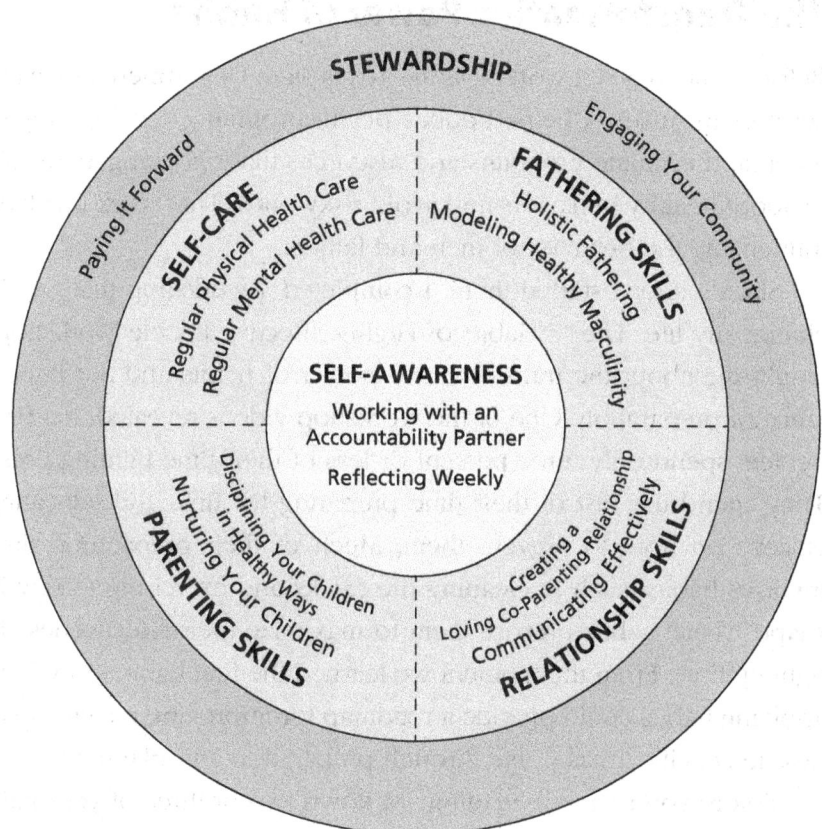

The system is anchored by the self-awareness habits on the front end because they're fundamental for following through on the remaining habits. The system is anchored by the stewardship habits at the back end because you'll apply them only after consistently applying the first 10. You can't pass on what you don't know, and you won't be ready to become a steward of confident fathering until you consistently apply the other habits first.

The Transformative Power of Habits

Before I joined NFI, I worked at the Texas State Department of Health Services in Austin. I helped public health programs develop, implement, and evaluate programs and resources that encouraged Texans to adopt healthy behaviors and avoid risky ones. That work involved influencing the behavior of men and fathers.

Shortly after I started there, I completed a workshop that would change my life. The "7 Habits of Highly Effective People Workshop" taught me about the transformative power of habits and the importance of preparation. One of the workshop videos revealed that firefighters spend only three percent or less of their time fighting fires.[1] They spend the rest of their time preparing for fires and educating citizens on how to prevent them. Much of their preparation time involves habits, such as cleaning fire trucks and exercising to stay in shape. These habits prepare them to maximize their effectiveness in fighting fires. From the moment we learned the first habit, I saw how applying habits could provide a roadmap for improving my effectiveness in specific areas of life through preparation and planning.

Before you continue reading, jot down two or three of your habits, things you do daily or weekly without fail. This is your first opportunity to use the worksheet at confidentfathers.com.

It might have taken you a moment to write down the habits because they're behaviors you repeat without thinking about them. Habits have the power to transform our lives in both positive and

---

[1]IARC Working Group on the Evaluation of Carcinogenic Risks to Humans. (2010). Exposure data. In *Painting, firefighting, and shiftwork* (IARC Monographs on the Evaluation of Carcinogenic Risks to Humans, No. 98). International Agency for Research on Cancer. https://www.ncbi.nlm.nih.gov/books/NBK326815/

negative ways. They can be friends or foes. People are sometimes unaware of their harmful habits. One of my harmful habits in raising my daughters was when I had differences with my wife in how to raise them. Rather than confront her and talk about the differences calmly, I retreated and buried my uncomfortable thoughts and feelings. That reaction prevented me from applying the habits of relationship skills (communicating effectively and creating a loving co-parenting relationship). In Chapter 6, you'll learn how I stopped that harmful habit.

Charles Duhigg is one of the country's foremost authorities on habits. In his book *The Power of Habit*, he says, "Most of the choices we make each day may feel like the products of well-considered decision making, but they're not. They're habits. And though each habit means relatively little on its own, over time, the meals we order, what we say to our kids each night, whether we save or spend, how often we exercise, and the way we organize our thoughts and work routines have enormous impacts on our health, productivity, financial security, and happiness." That's powerful. Duhigg cites a study by Duke University researchers that found more than 40 percent of our daily activities involve habits, rather than decisions.[2]

Researchers have extensively studied how habits function, particularly harmful ones. They have also explored ways to break those habits and replace them with healthier alternatives. We have gained substantial insights into how habits wire our brains, creating destructive behavior patterns, and how we can rewire them for healthier behaviors. I could discuss the research on habits for days; it's fascinating. However, I'll limit myself to three insights from the research that are most relevant to our work together.

---

[2]Duhigg, C. (2012). *The power of habit: Why we do what we do in life and business*. Random House.

Insight #1: Habits Put You on Autopilot

The first insight is how habits create behavior patterns that we repeat without thinking. They put us on autopilot: we don't have to think, we just act. When we establish habits, we reduce the "cognitive load" of thinking that requires energy.

According to Duhigg, the autopilot kicks in through a three-step process. First, something in your environment, known as the "cue," signals your brain to go on autopilot and perform a specific action, referred to as the "routine." When you perform the routine, you anticipate and crave the result or outcome that your brain likes or desires, known as the "reward."

Knowing how habits form is vital to implementing the 12 habits of a 24:7 Dad. Three characteristics of this loop are crucial to remember:

1. Each step—cue, routine, and reward—is essential. You can't establish a habit with only one or two.
2. The loop is self-reinforcing; once established, it sustains itself.
3. If you perform the loop frequently enough, it becomes a habit.

Parents use habits all the time. Take bedtime routines, for instance. At a specific time every night (cue), my wife and I bathed our girls, put them in pajamas, read to them, fed them, placed them in the crib, and turned off the light (routine). They got enough sleep, and so did we (the reward), at least on most nights!

Insight #2: Not All Habits Are Created Equal

Some habits are more powerful than others; they're called "keystone habits." Like the first domino in a lineup, which, when pushed, triggers all the other dominoes to fall one by one, these are the habits that matter more than others in behavior change. When you establish a keystone habit, it sets off a cascade of change. Exercise as part of caring for your physical health (Habit 3) is a prime example. The power of exercise lies not only in its ability to help people lose weight and become more fit, but also in its ability to start widespread, positive change in people's lives, even in areas that seem unrelated to physical fitness. As Duhigg points out, research shows that when people start exercising habitually, they usually eat better, smoke less, become more productive at work, exhibit greater patience, feel less stressed, and even use their credit cards less frequently. This cascading effect fosters other healthy habits because it makes them easier to establish.

Involved fathering leverages the power of keystone habits, which is why fathering affects so many people and areas of life. When men become involved fathers, it triggers a cascade of benefits for themselves, their children, mothers, and communities.

Insight #3: Habits Cueing Other Habits

The third insight is the power of "habit stacking." James Clear is one of the country's foremost authorities on habits. In his book *Atomic Habits*, Clear explains habit stacking as identifying a current habit and then stacking a new behavior on top. His habit-stacking formula is:

> "After [current habit], I will [new habit]."

The habits reinforce one another.[3] In other words, one habit cues you to perform another habit. Staying with the exercise as part of caring for your physical health, I work out first thing in the morning, but not every day. I exercise five to six days a week with one or two rest days. To help me maintain consistency with that weekly routine, I place my

---

[3]Clear, J. (2018). *Atomic habits: An easy & proven way to build good habits & break bad ones*. Avery.

exercise gear in a location where I'll see it the next morning. When I wake up, it reminds me that it's a workout day. Before the rest days, I don't lay out my gear. When I wake up the next morning, I know it's a rest day. The habit of laying out my exercise gear the day before made it easier to establish and maintain the routine because I didn't have to remember if it was an exercise or rest day. I stacked maintaining the routine on top of laying out my gear. (I also started recording the kind of workout I did right after I got home from the gym. That helped me maintain variety in my workouts, an important objective of mine.)

> ### Directing Your Rider
>
> *As I mentioned in the Introduction, getting the most out of this book involves trusting that research-backed habits and other guidance will work for you. One reason people don't change isn't a lack of motivation; it's a lack of clarity. They either lack guidance or the guidance they have is murky. I'll use research-backed information to provide you with clarity in establishing the 12 habits and addressing many of the pain points in fathering by "directing your rider."[4]*
>
> *In their book* Switch, *Chip and Dan Heath present a framework for helping people make difficult changes. Changing behavior requires appealing to people's emotional and rational sides. They refer to this as "motivating the elephant" (emotional) and "directing*

---

[4] In conducting extensive research, I prioritized the results of studies using a research methodology known as "meta-analysis." A meta-analysis combines separate studies on the same topic by statistically analyzing their combined data or results. This allows for a more reliable and precise estimate of an effect, such as the factors that lead to or cause a specific outcome. It increases statistical power, reduces bias, highlights consistent findings, and can help resolve conflicting results. This makes their conclusions more trustworthy.

the rider" (rational). Your elephant and rider must work together so that one doesn't override the other, and they move in the same direction.[5] Your elephant knows it wants to be a better father. You don't need me to motivate you. However, your rider needs a map to guide your elephant in the right direction. I'll provide that map.

Applying and Customizing the 12 Habits

Now that you understand how habits can help you, here's a framework that will help you apply and customize the 12 habits of a 24:7 Dad. Because there are many ways to apply each habit, I'll share seven options that will assist you in customizing the habits in a way that works for you, given your current stage in life and the fatherhood journey. These options will make applying the habits more manageable and help you focus on the most effective approaches for you. Using these options will help you identify ways to apply and customize the habits that are realistic rather than idealistic. By identifying realistic ways, you'll set yourself up for success. The options are:

- Ways that involve only me
- Ways that involve me and my children
- Ways that involve me and my co-parent
- Ways that involve my entire family
- Ways that involve one or more friends
- Ways that involve what I do at work or with co-workers
- Ways that involve me interacting with my community

---

[5]Heath, C., & Heath, D. (2010). *Switch: How to change things when change is hard.* Crown Business.

As you consider using these options, determine how your unique situation will affect the degree to which you can use them, such as the age of your children; whether or not you live with your children and have custody of them; the quality of the relationship with your co-parent; the quality of the relationship with your children; your employment status; whether you have a disability; and your overall physical and mental health status.

I recommend starting with two or three options that will provide the quick wins that are so helpful in forming and sticking with habits. You can refer back to these options when I ask you to customize the habits in each chapter.

When you customize each habit, I'll remind you to consider habit stacking. Here's an example of using habit stacking to customize the regular physical care habit in a way that involves a child: Suppose you're a divorced, non-residential father with partial custody of your nine-year-old son. You have him for the entire day every other Saturday. You've started exercising to improve your physical and mental health. You go to the gym most weekdays and try to do something active outdoors on the weekends. You want to firmly establish your weekend exercise routine. In choosing to involve your son in establishing this exercise routine, you decide that every other Saturday when he's with you, you'll take him on an outdoor adventure. This way, you stack the outdoor adventure habit with your exercise routine, making both habits easier to maintain.

Fathering Pain Points

As we discuss the knowledge, attitudes, and skills necessary for applying the habits, you'll learn how to address the challenges that fathers often face—not all of them, but those that research and the experiences of staff serving fathers in the organizations I've worked with identify as being among the most common. From now on, I'll use the term "pain points" rather than "challenges," "problems," or similar terms because they're often painful. Other terms don't carry the same connotation. You might have faced some of the pain points, depending on where you are in your fatherhood journey. If you have, you know they suck. These pain points include resolving conflicts, communicating effectively, how and when to discipline or punish your children, and more.

For example, in Chapter 4, you'll learn how to identify the traits of healthy masculinity that you want to pass on to your children. In Chapter 5, you'll learn to identify your typical style in disciplining your children and how to use non-violent discipline techniques. And in Chapter 6, you'll learn how to resolve rather than avoid conflicts with your co-parent and how to use the "Five-Second Rule" to communicate effectively with anyone. I'll describe each pain point and provide tips and other guidance on addressing it effectively.

Are you ready to learn and start applying the 12 habits to build the 6 traits? Let's do it.

Chapter 2

Self-Awareness: Accountability & Reflection

"Self-awareness gives you the capacity to learn from your mistakes as well as your successes. It enables you to keep growing."
—Lawrence Bossidy, retired CEO of Honeywell International

I spent a lot of time wandering around my hometown as a child. Not too far from my house were several car dealerships, and one of them had a storage shed behind it. As far as I could tell, it was always locked.

One Sunday, two of my friends visited the shed and found it was unlocked. Since the dealership was closed that day, they ventured inside and found a collection of items you wouldn't necessarily expect to see there, including a Yamaha motocross motorcycle. They thought it would be a good idea to gather a few friends, return to the shed, and take it.

The friend who arrived at my house didn't share exactly why he came by, only that he and our other friend had "something cool" to show me. I followed him to a spot near the dealership where we met our other friends. When they told me they wanted to steal some stuff from the shed, I hesitated until another friend said he wanted the motorcycle. I was in sixth grade at the time and had learned to ride my best friend's motorcycle and loved it. (He wasn't part of this burgeoning group of criminals.) My friend said he would store the bike and I could ride it if I helped him steal it. I wanted a motorcycle of my own—and of course my parents refused to buy me one—so I agreed.

We took the motorcycle to my friend's house, where he hid it from his parents. We rode it happily for several weeks until one day his parents noticed the motorcycle and questioned him about it. He told them he was keeping it for a friend, but they didn't believe him. He called me and asked if I could store it for a few days until the heat died down. I told him no, but he drove it to my house anyway, propping it against one of the sides without telling me.

One of my neighbors noticed it and called the police. They knocked on my door, and my mother answered. After they told her that the motorcycle had been stolen, she brought me to the door. The officer was a tall, burly, and intimidating sergeant. He asked if I knew anything about the motorcycle. I said I didn't know whose it was. He said if I knew something, I should call him or come down to the station. He left his card with us, took the motorcycle, and returned it to the dealership.

I've watched enough crime dramas to know he probably suspected I was involved, or at least knew something about who might have stolen it. I debated calling him because I didn't want to accept the consequences or throw my friends under the bus. I talked with my friends and tried to convince them we should come clean, but they refused. After a couple of weeks and discussions with my mother about my struggle, I eventually went down to the station.

The sergeant wasn't as intimidating this time. Maybe it was because he was sitting down instead of towering over me like he had in our doorway. Perhaps I had time to process the initial discussion with him. Regardless, I had resolved to come clean about my role. I didn't mention my friends' involvement (he already knew who was involved anyway). Amazingly, he said they wouldn't charge me! When I asked why, he explained that I was the first to come forward and confess. I'll never forget that sergeant. He held me accountable for my actions with patience, kindness, and compassion.

That's what this chapter is about: self-awareness, reflecting on your actions, and being accountable for them. Up to this point, I've asked you only a few reflection questions. Now, our journey picks up speed, and I'll be asking you to complete many reflective statements and questions from here on out. I'll also ask you to complete a deep-dive activity. Grab a notebook or notepad, and something to write with. If you'd rather have a worksheet to write on, you can download and print the one from confidentfathers.com by entering the URL into a search engine or scanning the QR code at the end of the Introduction.

Trait: Self-Awareness

A 24:7 Dad knows himself well—his moods, his strengths, and where he struggles. He understands how important he is to his family and owns his behavior completely. His growth as a father hinges on self-acceptance and recognizing that the choices he makes directly impact his ability to be there for his children. And he reflects regularly on how well he's fulfilling his fathering role.

Self-awareness is the most important of the 6 traits because it plays a pivotal role in behavior change, the foundation for the other 5 traits. People won't voluntarily change behavior if they're unaware that they need to do so. I learned this firsthand early in my tenure with National Fatherhood Initiative® (NFI), talking with fathers involved in the child welfare system and staff in the organizations supporting them with our programs. (Many of the fathers had their children removed from their homes and were trying to reunite with them.)

I wanted to know what motivated fathers to enroll in our programs and what kept them coming back. To my surprise, most of the fathers didn't enroll because they wanted to become better fathers. They enrolled because the organizations offered one or more resources that helped them meet immediate needs, such as obtaining their driver's license, securing housing, or finding a job. It wasn't until they'd been in our programs for a few weeks that they realized how much they didn't know about being good fathers. Only then did they become motivated to learn, which is what kept them coming back.

Some fathers don't realize that they need to be better fathers or, even if they do, the extent of improvement necessary. This lack of awareness is a barrier to change. Studies on self-awareness show its significance to a person's willingness to change.[1] Self-awareness is vital for the intrinsic motivation and goal setting that are crucial for maintaining change.[2] It also helps develop confidence around specific tasks and closes the gap between a person's actions and ideals.[3]

If you're not aware that you need to be a better father, you won't have the desire to change or maintain change, develop fathering confidence, or take the time to plan for how to be the father your children need you to be. To achieve self-awareness in your fathering, you'll need to implement two habits: working with an accountability partner and weekly reflection on your actions.

---

[1] Galleno, L., & Liscano, M. (2013). Revitalizing the self: Assessing the relationship between self-awareness and orientation to change. *International Journal of Humanities and Social Science, 3*(16, Special Issue), 64–65.

[2] Gillison, F. B., Rouse, P., Standage, M., Sebire, S. J., & Ryan, R. M. (2019). A meta-analysis of techniques to promote motivation for health behaviour change from a self-determination theory perspective. *Health Psychology Review, 13*(2), 109–143.

[3] Rhee, K., & Sigler, T. (2024). Can you develop self-awareness? Only if you are willing. *Journal of Leadership Education.* https://doi.org/10.1108/JOLE-02-2024-0045

Habit: Working with an Accountability Partner

Being held accountable means there's an expectation you might need to justify your actions or your failure to act when you should have. When I sat across from the police sergeant, I had to explain why I hadn't come forward sooner. You've undoubtedly been held accountable, whether by a family member, friend, or co-worker. Likewise, you've likely held someone else accountable. Take a minute to reflect on those interactions and complete the following statements:

- The last time someone held me accountable was _____.
- The person who held me accountable was _____.
- The last time I held someone accountable was _____.
- The person I held accountable was _____.

Think about the person who held you accountable. Did you ask them to do that? Now consider the person you held accountable. Did they ask you to do it? Most likely, your answers to both questions are no. Many people don't ask to be held accountable, which is unfortunate because more of us could really benefit from having accountability partners. Several factors contribute to establishing and maintaining accountability.[4] Four of them are particularly important for establishing this habit:

- The presence of another person
- Clarity around what's expected and agreement about the value of what's expected

---

[4] Mohr, D. C., Cuijpers, P., & Lehman, K (2011). Supportive accountability: A model for providing human support to enhance adherence to eHealth interventions. *Journal of Medical Internet Research, 13*(1), e30.

- Monitoring of compliance with what's expected
- Partners see each other as credible and legitimate

An accountability partner provides the presence—two people assisting or coaching each other to follow through on one or more commitments. This type of peer support improves individual and organizational performance by increasing the commitment to personal goals.[5] This support helps men in various ways, including making improvements in physical activity and addressing mental health challenges, as well as providing safety by increasing men's comfort in discussing their overall health challenges.[6,7] The effectiveness of peer support suggests that when you select an accountability partner, you should strongly consider other men and fathers. In addition to the pledge that I asked you to create at the end of the Introduction, choosing an accountability partner is another public commitment to becoming a 24:7 Dad. You'll reflect on potential accountability partners later.

To leverage the other three factors, the relationship can't be a one-way street. It must be a partnership of equals, with both parties benefiting from the relationship. That doesn't mean you benefit in

---

[5]Stewart, V. R., Snyder, D. G., & Kou, C.-Y. (2021). We hold ourselves accountable: A relational view of team accountability. *Journal of Business Ethics, 183*(3), 691–712.

[6]Sharp, P., Spence, J. C., Bottorff, J. L., Oliffe, J. L., Hunt, K., Vis-Dunbar, M., & Caperchione, C. M. (2020). One small step for man, one giant leap for men's health: A meta-analysis of behaviour change interventions to increase men's physical activity. *British Journal of Sports Medicine, 54*(20), 1208–1216.

[7]Sharp, P., Zhu, P., Ogrodniczuk, J. S., McKenzie, S. K., Seidler, Z. E., Rice, S. M., & Oliffe, J. L. (2024). Men's peer support for mental health challenges: Future directions for research and practice. *Health Promotion International, 39*(3), daae046.

the same way. You can hold each other accountable for different things, as long as the relationship is mutually beneficial. However, if you hold each other accountable for following through on actions in the same category, like fathering, it makes working with a partner easier, more motivating, and more sustainable.

Quick Win: Successful Accountability Partnerships

When forming any habit, using simple tactics that don't require much time to apply is beneficial. These "quick wins" will keep you motivated, especially since developing a habit can take a considerable amount of time.

Your first quick win is learning the factors that contribute to successful accountability partnerships. The factors are:

- **Complementary skills and perspectives.** Choose someone who sees things differently from you.[8,9]
- **Mutual buy-in.** Choose someone who is as committed to change as you are.[10]

---

[8]Reynolds, A., & Lewis, D. (2022, July–August). Teams solve problems faster when they're more cognitively diverse: Implications for accountability partnerships. *Harvard Business Review, 95*(4), 104–113.

[9]Burke, C. S., & Sims, D. E. (2017). The role of shared mental models and shared displays in team performance: Implications for organizational accountability partnerships. *Journal of Organizational Behavior, 38*(5), 731–752.

[10]Hoffman, A. J., Gillespie, J. J., & Wade-Benzoni, K. A. (2019). The science of cooperation and collaborative accountability. *Academy of Management Annals, 13*(2), 704–733.

- **Trusting and safe environment.** Choose someone you trust to keep discussions confidential and judgment-free.[11]
- **Constructive feedback.** Commit to honest and constructive feedback with transparency and avoid judging each other.[12]
- **Regular meetings.** Meet weekly for maximum effectiveness in sticking to your change objectives.[13]
- **Clear objectives.** Establish measurable goals and create statements for each one, ensuring you agree on what they mean.[14,15]

These factors can simplify deciding who might be a good partner and assist both of you in building a mutually beneficial relationship.

Customizing the Habit

It's time to customize the first habit on your journey toward becoming a 24:7 Dad! Selecting an accountability partner involves reflecting on one very important question: Who will be my accountability partner?

---

[11]Mohr, D. C., Cuijpers, P., & Lehman, K. (2011). Supportive accountability: A model for providing human support to enhance adherence to eHealth interventions. *Journal of Medical Internet Research, 13*(1), e30.

[12]Ryan, R. M., & Deci, E. L. (2017). *Self-determination theory: Basic psychological needs in motivation, development, and wellness.* Guilford Publications.

[13]Petersen, J. M., Prichard, I., Kemps, E., & Tiggemann, M. (2020). The effect of accountability partner presence and check-in frequency on goal adherence and weight management. *Health Psychology, 39*(7), 605–613.

[14]Locke, E. A., & Latham, G. P. (2019). The development of goal setting theory: A half century retrospective. *Motivation Science, 5*(2), 93–105.

[15]Prestwich, A., Kellar, I., Parker, R., MacRae, S., Learmonth, M., Sykes, B., & Castle, H. (2016). How can self-efficacy be increased? Meta-analysis of dietary interventions and accountability partnerships. *Health Psychology Review, 10*(2), 187–203.

An accountability partner can be someone other than your co-parent, such as a friend, co-worker, brother, cousin, or faith leader. Since it's ideal to work with another father who wants to be held accountable for his fathering, start your search there. Because your situations are different, you'll likely have different fathering objectives. As you consider whom to ask, keep in mind the first four factors that contribute to successful accountability partnerships you learned in the previous section. Your accountability partner should possess complementary skills and perspectives, be as committed to change as you are, create a trusting and safe environment, and offer constructive feedback.

If you can't think of another father to ask, it's fine to have someone else in mind who wants you to be their accountability partner in a different area of their life. The important thing is to have a mutually beneficial relationship with someone you know is dedicated to a partnership that meets the four factors. This work is too important to leave up to chance by trying to work with someone you're uncertain will share the same level of commitment to the relationship.

Meeting with Your Partner

Customizing this habit and the others is where the rubber meets the road. After securing an accountability partner, decide how often to meet and for how long (you don't have to meet in person). I recommend starting weekly or bi-weekly for the first two to three months; this is often enough to establish a solid foundation for the relationship. Then let the objectives each of you have for your fathering guide the frequency of your meetings. For example, if both of you have objectives to accomplish monthly, a monthly meeting will suffice. Choose a meeting length that's comfortable and convenient for both of you. Meetings don't have to be lengthy; 15 minutes may be sufficient for covering both sets of objectives.

Your meetings can be either informal or formal. Regardless, follow these guidelines for conducting effective accountability partnership meetings[16]:

- Create a standard agenda that begins with a review of your progress toward achieving your fathering objectives. I recommend reciting the commitment pledge (promise) mentioned in Chapter 1 at the start or end of the meeting.
- Prepare for future meetings by writing down your progress on your fathering objectives and the actions you agreed to take.
- Discuss your current struggles and what you've learned about overcoming them. If you and your partner face the same struggles, try to identify shared solutions.
- Help each other plan the steps you'll take before the next meeting and hold each other accountable for completing them.
- Review your standard agenda and, if necessary, adjust it before the next meeting.

After a few months of meeting with your accountability partner, discuss how well the meetings are helping both of you and whether you need to change anything about them.

---

[16] I drew on the following sources for these guidelines: 1) FICP. (n.d.). *Communicating with influence requires an accountability partner*. https://www.ficpnet.com/Blog/Article/communicating-with-influence-requires-an-accountability-partner; 2) Guynan, G. (2024, February 14). *Accountability partners: Don't achieve your goals alone!* Duke Recreation. https://recreation.duke.edu/story/accountability-partners-dont-achieve-your-goals-alone/

Habit: Weekly Reflection on Your Actions

Self-reflection is crucial for raising awareness about your fathering. If you have an existing reflective practice, work fathering reflection into it or create a separate time specifically for fathering reflection. If you're expecting your first child and don't have a reflective practice yet, start one weekly so you can include fathering once your child arrives. Even now, you can reflect on how well you're supporting the mother during her pregnancy. If you can reflect more often than weekly, that would be even better.

To get your reflection juices flowing, complete the following statements:

- The last time I reflected on an aspect of my life was _____.
- The reason I reflected on it was _____.
- I reflected on it by _____.
- Reflecting helped me by _____.

If you had difficulty completing those statements, remember that reflection takes many forms. Some forms, like meditation and journaling, are excellent for deep, structured reflection practiced consistently. Perhaps you've built such a reflection practice into your life. Other forms are more spontaneous, like taking a walk outside, calling a friend, or simply stepping away from your desk for a few minutes to think about a work issue. You're likely to have reflected on something in some way recently.

Reflecting on the 6 Traits

The 24:7 Dad carves out the time he needs to reflect on how effectively he's building the 6 traits. Fathers who participate in NFI programs learn to consistently ask themselves questions related to each characteristic. Make asking these questions a part of your fathering reflection:

- How well do I know myself?
- How well do I care for myself?
- How well do I father?
- How well do I parent?
- How well do I relate to others?
- How well do I help others with fathering?

As you reflect on those questions, consider how well you've applied each of the 12 habits that help build the 6 traits. While it might seem odd to reflect on how effectively you reflect, it's not. It's easy to skip a reflection session or spend too little time on reflection. Asking your accountability partner to ensure you regularly engage in reflection is just as vital as any other habit.

Quick Win: Journaling for Reflection

A quick win for the reflective habit is to write your thoughts in a journal on a daily basis. Journaling is a simple tool for recording your reflections on how well you're applying the 24:7 Dad's habits and developing his traits. I started journaling daily in 2020. It's helped me immensely in three ways: (1) processing my feelings and emotions on the same day I experience them; (2) making decisions in various aspects of my personal and professional life; and (3) holding myself accountable.

People journal to improve their mental health with good results;[17] it's a common partner of pharmacological treatments. Journaling

---

[17]Sohal, M., Singh, P., Dhillon, B. S., & Gill, H. S. (2022). Efficacy of journaling in the management of mental illness: A systematic review and meta-analysis. *Family Medicine and Community Health, 10*(1), e001154.

helps with accepting thoughts instead of judging them, resulting in fewer negative emotions. It also helps improve physical health, including blood pressure and liver and lung function, resulting in fewer sick days from work. And it can shorten the time it takes to find another job after losing one.[18,19,20]

Of course, you don't have to be in poor physical or mental health or have lost a job to benefit from journaling. Writing out your reflections can help you create the mental space to separate from and accept your feelings, allowing you to commit to being the best father you can be. There's no right or wrong way to record your thoughts. Your journal can be a beautiful notebook tailored for journaling or a composition notebook like the one I use, which is designed for writing essays or taking notes in school. If you prefer typing, you can create a document on your computer or phone. Record whatever comes to mind—use complete sentences, bulleted lists, jargon, acronyms, or any other method you're comfortable with. What's important is whatever helps you put pen to paper or keystroke to an electronic document on a regular basis.

Journaling regularly is a habit that makes reflecting on a weekly basis easier to establish and maintain. That's habit stacking! To establish journaling as a habit, use the three-step process you learned about in Chapter 1: cue, routine, and reward. Remember that you

---

[18]Sohal, M., Singh, P., Dhillon, B. S., & Gill, H. S. (2022). Efficacy of journaling in the management of mental illness: A systematic review and meta-analysis. *Family Medicine and Community Health, 10*(1), e001154.

[19]Ford, B. Q., Lam, P., John, O. P., & Mauss, I. B. (2018). The psychological health benefits of accepting negative emotions and thoughts: Laboratory, diary, and longitudinal evidence. *Journal of Personality and Social Psychology, 115*(6), 1075–1092.

[20]Baikie, K., & Wilhelm, K. (2005). Emotional and physical health benefits of expressive writing. *Advances in Psychiatric Treatment, 11*(5), 338–346.

can't establish a habit with only one or two of those steps. My journaling habit involves placing my journal in the kitchen after I finish my workday, which serves as the cue. For the rest of the day, I see the journal and anticipate recording my thoughts and experiences. When I write down my thoughts (the routine), I gain the pleasure and satisfaction of doing so (the reward). The reward feels even sweeter when journaling leads to an insight or a decision. It's usually the last thing I do before going to bed.

Customizing the Habit

Compared to the accountability habit, customizing a weekly reflection habit might be even easier because it involves only you. Reflecting on the following questions will help you customize this habit in a way that will work for you:

- How will I reflect weekly?
- When will I reflect weekly?

Around the time I started journaling, I also began meditating as a means of reflection and relaxation. (It also helps me enter a calm state to start my workday.) The process I used to establish this habit was:

- **Cue.** Arrive home from the gym.
- **Routine.** Go to my office, close the door, and either sit in my chair or lie down on the floor and start meditating.
- **Reward.** Relaxation and putting myself in a positive, calm state to start my workday.

Did you notice what else I did to establish that habit? I habit stacked! I stacked meditating onto the habit of exercising first thing in the morning. Consider linking your weekly reflection to another habit you do before or after it.

If you think that multiple ways of reflecting might work and aren't sure which will be most effective, experiment with them before deciding. You can also reflect in various ways if they work equally well, but I recommend starting with a single method. This approach is easier for developing the behavior into a habit, since focusing on one way to reflect is more manageable.

Deep-Dive Activity

Before moving on to the next chapter, complete the activity below. It will raise awareness of what you value most as a man and a father. (If you'd rather have a worksheet to write on, use the one from confidentfathers.com.)

Self-Awareness: Core Values

To raise your awareness of the man and father you want to be and model for your children, follow these steps:

1. Identify up to six action-oriented values that define the type of man and father you strive to be. A value is something very important to you, something that has worth. A core value is one that guides you in everything you do. You don't have to live the values right now. Use a verb to start each one. For example, two of mine are "commit to what matters most" and "practice self-compassion and compassion for others."

2. Capture your list in a way that will be easy for you to access it regularly. That might be typing and printing it to tape on a wall, writing it on a sticky note to place on your bathroom mirror, or putting it in an app on your smartphone.

3. After you finish this book, return to your list. Reflect on what you learned and whether you should update your values. Finalize your list.

After identifying your core values, read them regularly. Better yet, memorize them. A great time to read them is at the start of your weekly reflection. I read mine every morning after I meditate. Now I recite them from memory alongside quotes and reminders of mental models (valuable ways of thinking) that I've also memorized. The quotes and reminders keep me grounded and focused on what matters most to me. (You'll learn more about mental models in Chapter 6.) You can also ask your accountability partner to help you act in ways that align with your values.

AI Prompts

You can use AI tools in many creative ways to apply the 12 habits. A prompt is a set of instructions that you give the tool to generate the outcome you want. Use clear, detailed commands or questions in your prompts. Prompting "recipes" that use specific elements (ingredients) to instruct an AI tool are helpful. I used two simple recipes to create the hypothetical prompts throughout this book: the "role recipe" and "steps recipe." You can use these recipes to create your own prompts. The recipes are:

- **Role recipe.** Start with the role you want the AI tool to play and any experience the tool has in that role. Follow those ingredients with the outcome you want. Follow those ingredients with any factors for the AI tool to consider in generating the outcome.
- **Steps recipe.** Start with the outcome you want. Follow that ingredient with any factors for the AI tool to consider in generating the outcome. Follow that ingredient with "Provide a sequence of steps for me to follow."

Here are two hypothetical prompts I created for working with an accountability partner and reflecting weekly. These are only examples of how AI can be helpful in identifying ways to apply both habits.

- **Accountability.** Acting as a time-management specialist with experience advising people on how to collaborate, recommend criteria for deciding on a bi-weekly meeting schedule for two working fathers who will be each other's accountability partners. The partners will hold each other accountable for their respective fathering objectives.
- **Reflection.** I want to establish a consistent weekly self-reflection schedule. I know that I have time to reflect before going to work in the morning and after I put my two children to bed. Provide a sequence of steps for me.

For the working with an accountability partner habit, the AI tool I used recommended five criteria for creating the bi-weekly meeting schedule, which addressed consistency, timing, location, and format, alignment with "parenting rhythm," and practical considerations, such as creating a process for rescheduling cancelled meetings. For the reflecting weekly habit, the AI tool recommended 20 steps for establishing a weekly reflection schedule divided into four phases: preparation, implementation, sustainability, and integration.

To learn more about using effective prompts with AI, you can download a short list of resources at confidentfathers.com by entering the URL into a search engine or scanning the QR code at the end of the Introduction.

Chapter 3

Self-Care: Physical & Mental Health

"I found that with depression, one of the most important things you can realize is that you're not alone. You're not the first to go through it, you're not gonna be the last to go through it."
—Dwayne "The Rock" Johnson, wrestler and actor

The socialization of American men to ignore taking care of their physical health begins early. During my daughter Alexis's first soccer game when she was four years old, the mother of a boy playing in that game stopped him from leaving the field after he injured his knee. The boy started limping to the sideline. His mother rushed onto the field and compelled him to continue playing, despite his complaints and cries that his knee hurt. She told him to "suck it up."

Boys are not only expected to suck it up physically but mentally as well. The father of one of the other boys playing in that same game ceaselessly berated his son for choosing not to participate. The boy turned to his father looking for comfort, but his father refused to hold him. The boy cried. The father yelled at him to stop crying. The boy continued trying to connect with his father in the only way he knew how: for his father to hold him. His father spurned him again and again, berating the boy for crying instead of playing. The father lashed out, "We signed you up for soccer, and you will play!" The boy turned to his older sister. He sat in her lap as she wrapped her arms around him. When the father saw this, he screamed, "Let him go! Don't show him any pity!" The daughter let go and left the boy to cry alone. This boy was only four years old.

The socialization of boys to bury their physical and mental pain originates from the belief that it will help them grow up to be strong, courageous men. This belief runs so deep that it can lead people to ignore the impact of childhood trauma. In my early years with National Fatherhood Initiative® (NFI), I watched news coverage recounting the horrific story of a man who entered an Atlanta home, killing all the members of a family except for a 10-year-old boy. The boy locked himself in an upstairs closet to escape the carnage. The police found him while searching the home. Outside the home where paramedics examined the boy, a reporter interviewed the minister of the church the boy's family attended. When asked how the boy held up through this tragedy, the minister said, with his face and voice full of pride, "If he wasn't a man before, he sure is now!" I was appalled that this minister likened the tragedy to a rite of passage into manhood.

In this chapter, you'll learn to apply the two habits that are the most difficult for many fathers: regular physical and mental health care. I'd argue they're also the most crucial. That's why I'll provide plenty of guidance and tips in covering how vital it is to care for your physical and mental health, and how to address some of the pain points that can impact them the most.

Trait: Self-Care

The 24:7 Dad is a model of self-worth through his healthy choices; he understands the link between his physical and mental well-being. He prioritizes caring for his whole health by scheduling annual check-ups, eating nutritious foods, exercising regularly, reducing the impact of stress, and seeking knowledge about the world around him. When he needs help with his physical or mental health, he asks for it. And he fosters a strong bond with his family and community, surrounding himself with friends who encourage his healthy lifestyle.

As you learned in the Preface: Boys, Balls, and Backyards, I enjoyed physical activity growing up. In addition to playing sports, I was always outside, exploring the neighborhood and town on foot or on my bicycle—and for a brief time, on a stolen motorcycle! As I exited my teens, I started cross-training and became a gym rat. You can find me at 4:30 or 5:00 a.m. five days a week, just a few miles from home, strength training, using cardio machines, and darting around doing Tabata. I also enjoy yard work, particularly landscaping. I've always eaten well and have been diligent about getting annual physical health check-ups and blood work.

You also learned that I struggled at times with my mental health growing up. I've also struggled with it as an adult, including a specific mental health struggle that I'll share later in this chapter (along with what I did to address it).

If you don't establish the habits of regular physical and mental health care, you won't adequately care for your whole self in a way that helps you to be the best father for your children. The purpose of this chapter is to help you apply and customize these habits. In doing so, I'll discuss the pain points that fathers can face integrating regular physical and mental health care, such as staying physically active and expressing emotions and feelings in healthy ways.

Habit: Regular Physical Health Care

The state of a father's physical health affects his ability to be the best father possible. A father's premature death due to poor health cuts short the time children have with him. If he's physically unable to be active with his children, it limits what they can do together. For most men, being honest about their physical health care is the easier of the two self-awareness habits to address. It lacks the stigma and outright fear that accompanies mental health care, which we'll discuss later in this chapter.

Let's start by completing a few reflective statements about the state of your physical health and how you care for it:

- On a scale from 1 to 10, with 1 being "very poor" and 10 being "very good," I rate my overall physical health as a _____.
- One thing I can do to improve my physical health is _____.
- The last time I had an annual check-up for my physical health was _____.
- When I feel sick, I usually _____.

If you've taken great care of your physical health, congratulations! You've got this habit on autopilot. But if you haven't, you undoubtedly know you're not alone. A key to understanding the state of a man's physical health lies in how they were raised. Boys and men from all cultures learn a set of instructions that create a model of masculinity that dictates what a man and a father should be. In many cases, these instructions tell boys and men to bury and ignore their physical problems. By the time men become fathers, they've learned to deny the signs of ill health and that seeking help is a sign of weakness. Like the old Timex watch tagline, men learn that their bodies should "take a licking and keep on ticking." This leads men to mistreat their bodies and ignore warning signs that indicate they need help. Men often ignore the signs for so long that it's too late by the time they finally go to the doctor.[1,2]

---

[1]Mahalik, J. R., & Dagirmanjian, F. R. B. (2018). Working men's constructions of visiting the doctor. *American Journal of Men's Health*, *12*(5), 1582–1592.
[2]Cleveland Clinic. (2019, September 4). *Cleveland Clinic survey: Men will do almost anything to avoid going to the doctor*. https://newsroom.cleveland-clinic.org/2019/09/04/cleveland-clinic-survey-men-will-do-almost-anything-toavoid-going-to-the-doctor

The State of Men's Health

One of the reasons for helping you and other fathers to grasp the importance of physical and mental self-care is the poor state of men's health in America. While fathers tend to live longer than men without children, they also live an average of five years less than women. The death rate for men exceeds that of women for 9 of the 10 leading causes of death. Ninety-two percent of work-related deaths and 70 percent of alcohol-induced deaths are among men. There are many other differences too numerous to mention.[3]

For men of color, the picture is even worse, especially for Black men. The life expectancy for Black men is seven years shorter than that of white men. The death rate for Black men surpasses the death rate for American men of other races and ethnicities. Compared to white men, Hispanic and Native American men lose more years of potential life to chronic liver disease or cirrhosis of the liver, diabetes, and homicide.

Staying Physically Active

The time a father devotes to his parenting role can conflict with his desire and time to care for his physical health. When I became a father, it was hard to find time for exercise. I expected it would be hard to exercise during the first few weeks of fatherhood. After all, I was learning to change lots of poopy diapers day and night and getting only a few hours of sleep! What I didn't realize was how hard it would be to re-establish my cherished exercise schedule, especially after my wife returned to work. Fortunately, I adjusted. I began using the gym at work during lunchtime so I could fulfill my

---

[3]Nuzzo, J. L. (2020). Men's health in the United States: A national health paradox. *The Aging Male, 23*(1), 42–52.

fathering duties before work and after returning home. On weekends, I exercised early in the morning before my wife and daughter woke up.

One of the odd things about becoming a father is its different impacts on men's physical health. On one hand, becoming a father leads many men to stop or reduce harmful behaviors, such as smoking and alcohol abuse. On the other hand, fathering can compete with your objective of being physically active. Men are more likely than women to show declining physical activity after they become parents.[4] Men may lose as much as five hours of activity after their first child and another three and a half hours with a second child. Not surprisingly, men's weight increases when they transition to fatherhood. Physical activity is more difficult for fathers living in challenging conditions that require a focus on survival or who are otherwise marginalized, such as living in neighborhoods with little or no space for physical activity.[5]

In addition to finding time, several other factors can contribute to fathers' declining physical activity. Those factors include feeling guilty or selfish about taking time to exercise, moving from exercise with others to solo exercise, paying for gym memberships and organized sports versus paying for the new expenses of parenting, and prioritizing work–family balance over personal exercise.[6,7]

---

[4]Roberts, A. D., & Greenberg, E. R. (2022). Parenthood and physical activity. In K. Fingerman, J. B. James, R. F. Rodgers, & T. Betancourt (Eds.), *Handbook of families and health* (pp. 55–72). Springer.

[5]Darroch, F. E., Oliffe, J. L., Gonzalez Montaner, G., & Webb, J. M. (2021). Barriers to physical activity for fathers living in marginalising conditions. *Men and Masculinities, 27*(1), 147–166.

[6]Lovett, E., & Smith, A. (2024). Mental health, declining physical activity and social connection during transitions into fatherhood in the UK. *International Journal of Environmental Research and Public Health, 21*(7), 890.

[7]Mailey, E. (2014, October 9). *Dads, not just moms, battle balancing work, family, exercise.* ScienceDaily.

Whether or not those factors apply to you, staying physically active is crucial for your well-being and your children's. The 24:7 Dad knows this. You undoubtedly know the physical benefits of being active, eating healthily, limiting alcohol, and avoiding smoking and drugs. However, many fathers are unaware of the connection between their physical activity and their children's well-being. *That connection starts even before children are born.* When fathers are physically active during the mother's pregnancy, their children are less likely to be born with congenital heart disease.[8] When fathers have good cardiovascular health during the mother's pregnancy, such as having normal blood pressure that can be positively influenced by regular exercise, their children often enjoy better cardiovascular health at six years of age, regardless of whether their children have known risk factors for poor cardiovascular health, such as a high body mass index.[9]

The benefits for children of physically active fathers continue as children get older. By the time they enter school, these children tend to be more physically active themselves, which reduces their risk of obesity.[10] They're less likely to suffer from anxiety, depression, and

---

[8] Atieh, O., Azzi, N. M. J., Lteif, G. J., Atieh, N. A., Germanos, N. Y., Grandjean, V., Yarkiner, Z., Saliba, Z., Fadous Khalife, M.-C., & Raad, G. (2025). Paternal peri-conceptional physical activity and the risk of congenital heart disease in offspring: A case-control study. *Andrology, 13*(1), 34–44.

[9] Miliku, K., Bergen, N. E., Bakker, H., Hofman, A., Steegers, E. A. P., Gaillard, R., & Jaddoe, V. W. V. J. (2016). Associations of maternal and paternal blood pressure patterns and hypertensive disorders during pregnancy with childhood blood pressure. *Journal of the American Heart Association: Cardiovascular and Cerebrovascular Disease, 5*(10), e003884.

[10] Erkelenz, N., Kobel, S., Kettner, S., Drenowatz, C., & Steinacker, J. M. (2014). Parental activity as influence on children's BMI percentiles and physical activity. *Journal of Sports Science and Medicine, 13*(3), 645–650.

behavioral problems and more likely to be social, have self-control, and enjoy better overall emotional well-being.[11]

Quick Win: Being Physically Active with Your Children

Now that you know why staying physically active is so crucial to being a 24:7 Dad and to your children's well-being, I want to give you a quick win to start applying the habit of regular physical health care by staying physically active: engaging in physical activities with your children. Instead of providing a list of activities, which you can easily find online, here are some steps to identify activities that are age-appropriate for each of your children and fit your circumstances:

- **Assess your child's physical abilities.** How are your child's motor skills, attention span, and ability to perform tasks independently? What is their typical energy level, and when is it lowest and highest? Do they have any physical limitations or specific interests?

- **Assess your physical abilities.** Ask yourself the same questions. Be truthful about your physical abilities and interests. Select activities you enjoy and can stick with.

- **Identify the resources at your disposal.** Note where you can perform indoor and outdoor activities, such as a spare room, your yard, parks, recreation centers, hiking trails, running tracks, and ball fields. Organize them by availability across the seasons. Aim for a balance between activities at home and those away.

---

[11]Davidson, G., Bunting, L., McCartan, C., Grant, A., McBride, O., Mulholland, C., Nolan, E., Schubotz, D., Cameron, J., & Shevlin, M. (2024). Parental physical activity, parental mental health, children's physical activity, and children's mental health. *Frontiers in Psychiatry, 15*, 1405783.

- **Consider your access to your child.** If you don't live with your child or have custody of them, it might limit how often you can engage in activities with them. If you don't live with your child and co-parent, you might need to discuss activities with your co-parent and obtain their approval.

- **Identify activities.** Use the Internet to find ideas for age-appropriate activities. Consult your child's doctor. Seek advice from parents with older children about what they did at that age. Look for community groups suited for your child's age, such as those at a library, recreation center, or gymnastics facility. Strive for a balance between structured (directed) and unstructured (free-flowing, child-led) activities.

- **Experiment, observe, and adjust.** Choose a few simple activities to test. How engaged is your child? Do they get frustrated or angry? Do they ask to do the same thing repeatedly? Do they get bored or overwhelmed because the activity is too hard? Tweak activities as you go. Take note of the activities that work well and try a few more. Keep testing until you have a handful of activities you both enjoy.

- **Create a schedule.** Set regular times for physical activity in your calendar or family calendar. If your child has their own calendar, encourage them to add these times as well. Decide whether to allocate some of the times for a specific activity—maybe one you do every week—or leave it open. If your child is old enough, involve them in the scheduling process. They'll be more committed if you do. Be flexible in changing days, times, and activities. When an activity starts to feel like a chore, it's time to move on.

- **Expand and change.** If you have time for more activities, add them. As your children age, change them. As they mature, they'll want to engage in more activities on their own or with friends. That's normal. Adjust your shared activities in response.

If you're married or living with your co-parent, include them in the activities and find ways they can participate while still allowing for personal time with your child. If you have other children, consider activities you can do solely with them as well as those that involve the whole family.

Supporting Your Co-Parent

Before turning to mental health care, let's address the importance of supporting your co-parent's ability to care for their physical health. In addition to participating in activities along with you and your child (or children), they might want space for activities that they enjoy doing alone or with others, like friends. Not only will supporting them respect their desire to start or stay physically active, it will provide time away from the family, which also aids in caring for their mental health. Discuss how you can support each other's physical activity. Creating a schedule for when each of you will engage in your respective activities can be helpful for managing expectations and avoiding misunderstandings, such as planning activities that conflict. Plus, it will earn you massive brownie points!

Customizing the Habit

It's time to customize how you'll care for your physical health regularly. This decision involves reflecting on the following questions:

- What have I learned so far in this chapter that will help me with regular physical health care?
- How will I take care of my physical health regularly?

In contrast to the self-awareness habits, which had clear options for customizing, choosing an accountability partner and reflecting weekly, customizing the physical health habit can involve any one or more of the seven customization options in Chapter 1 that work for you. If you think you've got this habit down—that you're already doing enough to care for your physical health—take this time to re-evaluate what you're doing. Keep doing what's working for you while considering the "buckets" framework below to identify other ways that can help you do an even better job. Simply reflect on the options that those ways represent and move on to learn about mental health care.

If you're starting from scratch in caring for your physical health—or simply want to improve upon what you're already doing—consider ways that fall into "prevention" and "intervention" buckets. The prevention bucket includes activities that prevent or reduce the risk of poor health, such as consistently exercising, eating more nutritious foods, and drinking more water. The intervention bucket is for activities that will repair poor health, such as going to the doctor when you get sick, taking your prescription medication regularly and as prescribed, and doing physical therapy exercises despite the pain. As you reflect on those two buckets, you could, for example, take a cooking class with a friend that's focused on preparing nutritious meals (prevention) or ask your co-parent to remind you to take your prescription medication (intervention).

Customizing this habit can involve not only starting new activities but also stopping behavior that is or could potentially damage your health (which could be more helpful than starting something new). Quitting smoking or use of smokeless tobacco, cutting out sugary drinks or alcohol, and giving up late-night television watching so you can go to bed earlier and get more sleep are examples.

And don't forget to consider habit stacking!

Habit: Regular Mental Health Care

The same model of masculinity that leads men to ignore signs of their physical needs also demands that they overlook and suppress most emotions. From a young age, boys learn that expressing emotions, especially those linked to pain and sadness, is a sign of weakness. Emotional men are often labeled as sissies or wimps. In fact, seeking help for mental health carries a stigma so great that many men fear reflecting on it, let alone discussing it with someone else.

Taking care of your mental health is just as much an ongoing requirement as your physical health. Mental health refers to the ability to adapt and cope with the demands of everyday life. Good mental health involves careful thinking, allowing you to adjust to and meet life's demands without harming yourself or others. Your mental health affects your physical health and vice versa.[12]

With that in mind, complete the following statements:

- On a scale from 1 to 10, with 1 being "very poor" and 10 being "very good," I rate my overall mental health as a _____.
- One thing I can do to improve my mental health is _____.
- The main causes of stress in my life are _____.
- The way I usually handle stress is _____.
- When I was a boy, I was taught that showing my feelings or emotions was _____.
- Today, I think that showing my feelings or emotions is _____.

Don't be surprised if you found it harder to complete these statements compared to those earlier in this chapter on your physical health. As I highlighted in the Preface: Boys, Balls, and Backyards, I had a hard time as a child expressing my feelings or emotions.

---

[12]Dubash, S. (2024). The interplay of depression symptoms and physical activity: Bidirectional insights from 25-years of the Americans' changing lives panel. *Mental Health and Physical Activity, 26,* 1–11.

I didn't know how to manage them. The sessions with my therapist were helpful, especially in overcoming odd tics I'd developed. In early adulthood, my work with Jon and the other men and fathers in healing the father wound was also beneficial. But I eventually drifted away from working with other men and fathers, thinking I had adequately addressed my past. I shifted my focus to building a career and the family life I didn't have growing up. But the trauma of my childhood ran deeper than I had imagined. Coupled with my reserved temperament, it continued to affect my mental health. I buried most of my feelings and emotions so deeply that I remained unaware of how much more work I needed to do. I rarely experienced joy, including the joy of fathering. At times, I was depressed and didn't even realize it.

The Summer of 2019

My focus striving to be the best father and husband I could be and on helping other fathers through my work with NFI created an impenetrable force field around my feelings and emotions. I didn't spend time on my well-being, apart from maintaining regular exercise and a healthy diet. Then came the summer of 2019, and everything changed. I began to feel uneasy, unnerved, and frightened. The force field I had created to keep my feelings and emotions at bay started crumbling. I couldn't pinpoint the cause and thought something was very wrong with me. I was sensing feelings and emotions, such as stress and sadness, more deeply than ever. I felt completely lost in explaining the reason for my failing force field, except for feeling a much heavier weight of responsibility than ever for the well-being of my family and NFI. I was unsettled by the intensity of my feelings and the emotional pain I felt. For the next few months, I tried to make sense of it all but couldn't, and I fought to maintain my force field.

In late 2019 and into early 2020, the crumbling of the force field accelerated. It converged with caring for two elderly parents, the isolation caused by the COVID-19 pandemic, and the transition from having my children at home to becoming an empty nester. I had managed my mother's financial affairs and ensured her physical care for many years. In December 2019, I also took on the same financial-management role for my father, with my wife supporting his physical care. His life was chaotic, and his finances and health were in disarray after years of neglect. Over four and a half long, painful years, taking care of him turned my life (and my wife's life) upside down and reopened my father wound.

I eventually realized that the force field needed to crumble because it was preventing me from being as mentally healthy as I wanted to be and from handling the life change I was going through. I let the force field complete its disintegration and sought help. I discovered action and commitment therapy, which focuses on healing from mental health challenges by changing how a person reacts and relates to their thoughts and emotions instead of trying to change those thoughts and emotions. I also entered therapy again for the first time since my childhood, working with a therapist who specializes in helping men. And I was supported by a loving, patient family and faith that God would give me the strength to heal.

My point in sharing that painful experience is to provide an example of how challenging it can be to care for your mental health and that fathers can overcome mental health challenges with help. If you're struggling with your mental health, I've been where you are. It's easy to lose sight of caring for your mental health, even after realizing how critical that care is and benefiting from it, as I did with the help of therapy earlier in my life. Life happens. Work, parenting, and caring for others who can no longer care for themselves creeps in and, before you know it, you're struggling with your emotions and feelings. Getting the help you need, along with having faith that you can heal (no matter where that faith comes from), is the light at the end of the tunnel.

Men's inability or reluctance to express emotions frequently leads to physical and mental health issues. To raise healthy children, you must first recognize that expressing your emotions and connecting with them is manly. Additionally, you must learn to express your emotions appropriately. Anger is the emotion that society typically allows men to express. However, due to suppressing their other emotions, men sometimes display anger inappropriately, which can escalate into rage. This often occurs because anger is a secondary emotion that arises from unresolved loss and an inability or unwillingness to grieve. Suppressing emotions can also lead to depression. We'll discuss depression and grieving losses shortly. But first, let's turn our attention to the most common pain point for all parents, including fathers: parenting stress.

Stress/Stressors

Stressors are the factors in life that cause or contribute to stress, and stress contributes to mental health challenges. Parenting brings its own stressors that only add to the stressors of life without children. Fathers and mothers experience and deal with the impacts of that stress differently, but that's rarely acknowledged outside academic circles.

In the summer of 2024, then US Surgeon General Vivek Murthy raised the nation's awareness of parenting stress by calling attention to the increasing gap between the stress reported by parents compared to other adults, stress that results from the rigors of raising children today.[13] What was alarming was how much more stress

---

[13] Office of the Surgeon General. (2024, August 28). *Parents under pressure: The U.S. Surgeon General's Advisory on the mental health and well-being of parents.* https://www.hhs.gov/surgeongeneral/reports-and-publications/parents/index.html

parents today report having compared to when I raised my daughters. Even more alarming was the negative impact that increased stress is having on parents and how it affects children negatively. I was pleased to see that the advisory dedicated a section to fathers' parenting stress (and mother's parenting stress) and its impact on fathers' mental health and their children, such as how fathers' depression resulting from stress can have a negative effect on their children's behavior.

Depression

A friend's experience highlighted how fathers experience and react to parenting stress, and how fathers' and mothers' reactions to it can differ. He welcomed his second daughter into the world 16 years after his first. She was born eight weeks premature and weighed only four and a half pounds. As a result, she spent time in the neonatal intensive care unit (NICU). Fortunately, she was heavier and better developed than many preemies at that stage. She surpassed her birth weight fairly quickly, came off her feeding tube, and started breastfeeding. She came home after three months.

Having a baby in the NICU is tough on parents. It can impose harsh financial and emotional costs. Two notable emotional costs are stress and depression. You'd think that when parents bring their baby home from the NICU it would reduce their stress, but it doesn't. It stresses fathers more than mothers. Fathers' stress increases during the first two weeks at home, while mothers' stress remains constant.[14]

While I wasn't surprised to learn that preemies' fathers are stressed—my friend had been very stressed since her birth—the insight raised even more concerns about his well-being after she

---

[14]Garfield, C. (2017, December 4). *Preemies' dads more stressed than moms after NICU*. Northwestern University. https://news.northwestern.edu/stories/2017/december/preemies-dads-more-stressed-than-moms-after-nicu

came home. I worried about the potential long-term effects of his heightened stress, including depression. If he didn't acknowledge and manage his stress, it could become chronic. My friend might have faced the double whammy of stress and postpartum depression. (We've known for at least a decade that fathers can experience postpartum depression.[15]) Even if his daughter had been born full-term, he might have become depressed.

My friend's situation prompted me to reflect on NFI's work and how my new insight on stress and depression might help organizations serving fathers experiencing them (paternal stress and depression). I wondered about fathers' potential for paternal depression as their children grow older. I questioned whether fathers of older children experience paternal depression and, if so, how it might affect their children. It led me to the research of Craig Garfield, Associate Professor of Pediatrics and Medical Social Sciences at Northwestern University.

Garfield found that the first five years after a child's birth are the riskiest time for paternal depression. Young fathers, aged 25 and under, are especially at risk. Their depression increases by nearly 70 percent during a child's first five years.[16] In other research, Garfield found that depressed fathers are more likely to abuse or neglect their children, less likely to read to them, and less likely to engage with them overall. As a result, their children are more likely to face developmental delays and behavioral problems.[17] More recently, an

---

[15]Kim, P., & Swain, J. E. (2007). Sad dads: Paternal postpartum depression. *Psychiatry (Edgmont), 4*(2), 35–47.

[16]Garfield, C. F., Duncan, G. J., Rutsohn, J., McDade, T. W., Adam, E. K., & Coley, R. L. (2014). A longitudinal study of paternal mental health during transition to fatherhood as young adults. *Pediatrics, 133*(5), 836–843.

[17]Garfield, C. F., Isacco, A., & Chung, P. J. (2011). Fathers' depression related to positive and negative parenting behaviors with 1-year-old children. *Pediatrics, 127*(4), 612–618.

analysis of 84 studies revealed that children whose fathers were depressed, anxious, or stressed during the perinatal period have a higher risk of poor social-emotional, cognitive, language, and physical development.[18]

My investigation also led me to the work of researchers in the United Kingdom. They examined the effects of paternal depression on teenage children and found that, independent of maternal depression, paternal depression increases the risk of depression in teens.[19] Teenage depression can have dire consequences. Depressed teens are more likely to have problems in school, smoke, abuse alcohol and other drugs, attempt suicide, and be obese. The consequences of teenage depression don't fade away; they extend into adulthood. These teens are more likely to become adults with anxiety, bipolar disorder, suicidal behavior, and physical health problems. They're also more likely to be unemployed.[20]

The implication of this research is clear: *Every father, including you, must care for his mental health.* The 24:7 Dad knows this. Watch for the signs of depression in yourself and in the fathers you know.

---

[18]Le Bas, G., Aarsman, S. R., Rogers, A., Macdonald, J. A., Misuraca, G., Khor, S., Spry, E. A., Rossen, L., Weller, E., Mansour, K., Youssef, G., Olsson, C. A., Teague, S. J., & Hutchinson, D. (2025, June 16). Paternal perinatal depression, anxiety, and stress and child development: A systematic review and meta-analysis. *JAMA Pediatrics.* Advance online publication.

[19]University College London (UCL). (2017, November 16). *Teenage depression linked to father's depression.* UCL News. https://www.ucl.ac.uk/news/2017/nov/teenage-depression-linked-fathers-depression

[20]Thapar, A., Collishaw, S., Pine, D. S., & Thapar, A. K. (2012). Depression in adolescence. *Lancet, 379*(9820), 1056–1067.

Your well-being—and your children's—might depend on it. Symptoms in men can include[21]:

- Feeling hopeless
- Losing interest in activities you've enjoyed
- Difficulty focusing or concentrating
- Irritability, anger
- Aggressive and other risky behavior
- Increased alcohol and drug abuse

Don't let your pride or fear prevent you from seeking help for depression and other mental health challenges.

Loss and Grief

Loss is one of the stressors that men find the most difficult to express and manage and can lead to anxiety, depression, and other mental health issues.[22,23] Loss often becomes more devastating in fatherhood, such as when a child dies or a co-parent dies or abandons the family, leaving a father to raise his children alone.

---

[21]Mayo Clinic. (2024, February 13). *Male depression: Understanding the issues.* https://www.mayoclinic.org/diseases-conditions/depression/in-depth/male-depression/art-20046216

[22]Norman, N. (2022, November). *The problem of male grief.* Psychology Today. https://www.psychologytoday.com/us/blog/men-s-mental-health-matters/202211/the-problem-male-grief

[23]Mayo Clinic. (2022, December 13). *Complicated grief.* https://www.mayoclinic.org/diseases-conditions/complicated-grief/symptoms-causes/syc-20360374

It's crucial to process loss. Learning how starts with grasping the connection between loss and grief. Loss is a stressor that causes grief. It refers to no longer having something due to an accident, carelessness, separation, or death. You can lose things you can see, such as money, a home, a parent or child, or a business. You can also lose things you can't see, such as love, health, respect, and self-worth.

Grief is how humans respond to loss. The four stages of grief are denial of loss, sadness over it, anger about it, and, finally, acceptance of it. Reactions to loss vary based on the type of loss, the significance of what was lost, previous experiences with loss, and coping abilities. Depending on the nature of the loss and their willingness to cope with that loss, it can take a week, a month, a year, or even many years for a father to move through the grieving process. The challenge for most fathers is that they've never been taught how to grieve. They've learned instead that it's not manly to grieve so they often get stuck in the anger stage. They've been told to, "Take it like a man!," "Get over it!," and "Grow up!"

When men do grieve, they often do so differently than women.[24] Some of the ways men grieve are healthy, while others are unhealthy. Men frequently hide their grief instead of taking care of their emotions. They say things like, "It doesn't hurt that bad" or "I'm okay" to keep people away. They take time away or want to be alone to think things through. They show anger more often than sadness. They grieve through rituals, such as doing or making something.[25,26]

---

[24]Lundorff, M., Bonanno, G. A., Johannsen, M., & O'Connor, M. (2020). Are there gender differences in prolonged grief trajectories? A registered-sampled cohort study. *Journal of Psychiatric Research, 129*, 168–175.

[25]Jannsen, S. J. (2016, August). *Understanding the way men grieve.* Social Work Today. https://www.socialworktoday.com/archive/exc_0816.shtml

[26]Hurrott, S. (2023, December 20). *How men handle grief differently compared to women.* Banner Health. https://www.bannerhealth.com/healthcareblog/better-living/how-men-handle-grief-differently-compared-to-women

Crying is the most natural and primary tool humans have to grieve. It releases the energy of grief. Tears of sadness aren't the same as tears of joy. When your body signals it's time to cry and you resist crying, the energy emerges in other ways, such as anger and rage. Men learn at an early age that it's unmanly to cry. It's one of the lessons that damages men the most.[27]

Quick Win: Healthy Ways to Grieve

I'm giving you this quick win because grief is so hard for many men to express. Here are some healthy ways to grieve that you can use immediately to improve your mental health:

- Show courage and allow yourself to grieve instead of hiding your feelings
- Tell people when you need to be alone to think things through
- Don't shut others out
- Listen to your body and become aware of how it reacts to grief, such as feeling sick to your stomach or getting a headache
- Use rituals and activities to work through your grief, such as spending time outdoors
- Slow down and reflect on the cause of your grief
- Stay close to friends you can count on
- Stay in good health and continue exercising
- Cry if you need to

---

[27]Rice, S. M., Oliffe, J. L., Seidler, Z., Borschmann, R., Pirkis, J., Reavley, N., & Patton, G. C. (2021). Gender norms and the mental health of boys and men. *The Lancet Psychiatry, 8*(6), e541–e542.

The more often you use these options to address your grief, the easier it will be to grieve your losses and the more comfortable you'll feel about grieving in general.

Work–Family Balance[28]

Another common pain point and stressor for many fathers is balancing work and family due to the internal and external conflict it creates. As you learned in the Introduction, today's fathers place a high value on fathering and desire to spend time with their children. Fathers' work schedules, including non-traditional hours such as overnight shifts, can limit the time they have with their children. Generally, fathers express that they don't spend enough time with their children, often attributing this to work obligations. Fathers report more work–family conflict than mothers. Moreover, when fathers have work–family conflict, it's more likely to cause problems for children compared to when mothers have work–family conflict.

This conflict emerges from the moment working fathers welcome their children into the world because of the lack of paid paternity leave. For working fathers, the ability and willingness to take paternity leave when their children are born enhances the likelihood of long-term involvement. Taking paternity leave positively influences father involvement in general and specifically enhances father–infant bonding and fathering identity.

Unfortunately, the United States is one of the few developed countries that doesn't provide some form of paid paternity leave as a government benefit. That leaves employers to offer paid paternity

---

[28]Unless referenced otherwise, the facts in this section are supported by research included in the following publication: Brown, C., Trahan, M., Garnett-Deakin, A., Pond, E., Cho, S., & Gibson, S. (2024). *Father Facts 9*. National Fatherhood Initiative®.

leave or working fathers to fund it with their savings. While many US employers offer unpaid paternity leave, recent surveys indicate that a quarter or fewer of them offer paid paternity leave.

Nevertheless, the proportion of US fathers taking paternity leave—paid or not—has increased substantially due to the overall rise in employers offering any form of paternity leave and the increasing acceptability of fathers taking it. But when fathers take advantage of this benefit, they take very little of it and don't use all they're allotted.

While employer support of fathers is an important piece in solving fathers' work–family conflict, the more important piece is the strong relationship men have with work. Despite the importance that today's fathers place on being a father—more importance than they place on work success—men continue to find great meaning in their work. In fact, the importance that work plays in their identity increases when they become a father and as they have more children.[29,30] Think about it. What do most men talk about when they meet another man for the first time? Work!

Work should be very important to you, and you should gain a great deal of pleasure from it. It's vital for self-worth—just ask someone who has been out of work for a long time. Many fathers struggle because they allow work to control their lives to the point that they lose sight of how much they value family; they struggle to see the

---

[29]Meeussen, L., Veldman, J., & Van Laar, C. (2016, October 16). Combining gender, work, and family identities: The cross-over and spill-over of gender norms into young adults' work and family aspirations. *Frontiers in Psychology*, 7, 1781.

[30]Gaunt, R., & Scott, J. (2017). Gender differences in identities and their sociostructural correlates: How gendered lives shape parental and work identities. *Journal of Family Issues*, *38*(13), 1852–1877.

connection between work and family. Instead, they see themselves merely as financial providers or believe that providing financially is so essential that neglecting other forms of support is acceptable.

Work–family balance is crucial to being a 24:7 Dad. It starts with knowing what work–family balance truly means—fulfilling both work and family responsibilities. When you achieve this balance, it shows that you equally value work and family. Finding that balance isn't just about spending enough time with your family. To truly value family, you must value what your work provides for them. Likewise, to truly value work, you must value how your feelings about your family help to make you a better employee.

If you're unsure whether your work–family balance is out of line, ask yourself the following questions:

- Is success at work or success at home more important?
- Do I worry that if I try to balance work and family, my employer won't value me as much as they do now? If so, is this concern based in reality?
- If my employer offers benefits that can help me balance work and family, am I using them?
- When I'm home, am I maximizing the time I spend with family?
- When I'm home, how often do I work or think about work? If it's often, does this prevent me from focusing on time with my family? Is this fair to my family and me?
- Do I often work on weekends, holidays, and even during vacations? If so, does this keep me from focusing on time with my family? Is this fair to both my family and me?

What did your answers reveal? What changes can you make to find a better work–family balance?

Quick Win: Tips for Work–Family Balance

If your answers revealed that your work life is so consuming that your family life is suffering, it's time for action. To create better work–family balance on the work side of the equation, use the following tips:

- **Inform your co-workers about your family commitments.** Discuss your desire to balance work and family with your co-workers and boss. This will show them you prioritize family alongside your job.

- **Make your boss an ally.** That requires honesty, trust, and hard work. Work with them to create ways that help you balance your responsibilities at work and home. Document your job progress in a weekly report to your boss. This way, you're judged on your achievements, not just your attendance.

- **Stay busy and focused.** Complete your tasks during the day so you can spend time with your family in the evening. You can relax knowing you dedicated yourself to a full day of work.

- **Be a team player.** Offer to assist your co-workers and boss with special projects. It's a great way to show you can be flexible. Treat others the way you want to be treated, and they'll help you balance work and family.

- **Be thoughtful about special jobs.** Carefully reflect on the benefits and impact on family time before agreeing to overtime work or special assignments. While earning extra money or gaining respect can be tempting, those jobs may also lead to less time with family.

- **Show or share your children's artwork and family photos.** If you have an office or workstation, these visuals will remind you and your co-workers about your family commitment, but be careful not to overdo it. Three or four items will suffice.

If you don't have a place to display these visuals, put them on your mobile phone, if they're not there already, and share them.

- **Maintain a family commitment with the same energy you use to maintain a work commitment.** Avoid missing a family commitment due to an unexpected or unscheduled work request, such as a late-afternoon meeting scheduled at the last minute or an opportunity for overtime. If you feel that the work request is too important not to fulfill, immediately inform the family members affected and explain the reason for missing the commitment.
- **Use work benefits that assist you in balancing work and family.** Your employer may provide benefits such as flextime, shift swapping, telecommuting, parental or paternity leave, or leave banks. If your employer doesn't offer those benefits, consult your human resources office about potentially providing them.

To help you achieve better work–family balance on the family side of the equation, use the following tips:

- **Make career decisions as a family.** Ask your family members what they think about a new opportunity and how they'd feel if you accepted it.
- **Limit your work on weekends, vacations, and holidays.** Avoid making a habit of working during your days off. You need time away from work to focus on family. Have a co-worker cover your duties while you're on vacation. This will help you avoid worrying about work while you're away.
- **Spend time with your family every day.** Don't confine it to the weekends. Identify moments and activities during the week for family time. Tuck your children into bed, go for an evening

stroll, or simply share dinner or breakfast together. If you don't live with your children, spend as much time with them as possible. Discover ways to talk with them every day, whether by phone, email, or text.

- **Turn off your mobile phone and laptop during family time.** This tip applies to your work and personal devices. Don't let work emails or chats distract you from family time. Don't scroll through your social media feeds. The amount of screen time parents and children spend today is one of the major barriers to family members focusing on the time they spend together. It prevents parents and children from listening to each other and having emotionally intimate discussions and other interactions.

- **Create and sign a "family contract."** Ensure that your children and your co-parent sign it as well. State your goal to balance success at work with success at home so you can be a 24:7 Dad. Include specific commitments for family time. Review the contract at the beginning of each week to remind yourself of this commitment.

Another great tip is to use a shared family calendar where all family members can enter their most important personal commitments (family, school, and work) that other family members should know about. Focus on entering commitments that are out of the ordinary, such as a late work meeting or school event. A digital calendar like Google Calendar works best because of its flexibility in modifying commitments and adaptability as your family grows. At the start of each week, spend 15–30 minutes with your family members discussing your respective commitments, when someone might need help from another family member, such as picking up a child from daycare, and adding things you want to do together, such as a family dinner, movie night, or daytrip. Taking this time to plan allows each family member to modify their personal commitments as needed to ensure mutual support for each other and the family as a whole.

If you're struggling to make enough money to help support yourself or your family, some of these tips can seem unrealistic at first glance. If you're working two or three jobs, have overnight shifts resulting in less time with your family, or work for an employer or boss that doesn't care enough about their employees to help them balance work and family, your initial thought might have been, "These tips won't work for me." If you had that reaction, step back and put the tips in context. Look at each of these tips and ask yourself, "How can this tip work for me?" For example, if you have a mobile phone and you're not "on call," turn it off during the limited time you have with family. And when you're with family, identify ways to spend as much time with them as possible. Ask your co-parent for their input. If your children are old enough to help, ask for their input. Ask co-workers who are fathers if they have any advice. Anything you can do to move the needle toward better work–family balance will be worth it.

Quick Win: Tips for Overall Mental Health

I've already given you some tips for addressing two specific pain points related to mental health care: grieving and work–family balance. The following tips are for building a broader foundation that supports overall mental health. They include ways of thinking (the first four tips) and actions (the remaining tips) that you can quickly take:

- **Be grateful.** Each night before bed, make a list of three things you're thankful for. They can be general things you're grateful for or things that happened that day. Occasionally, share your list with a family member or friend.

- **Be patient.** Sometimes, the best way to deal with issues and stress is to remain patient and allow things to unfold naturally. Don't try to force solutions.
- **Get real.** Reflect on all the "shoulds," "woulds," "coulds," and "musts" in your life. Assess which ones are positive and worth keeping. Eliminate the negative ones.
- **Be content.** This is easier said than done. Focus on all the good instead of all the bad in the world. When you focus too much on the bad, you develop an unhappy view of people and their actions. Avoid complaining about things.
- **Eliminate clutter.** Life can become so busy that it spirals out of control. Create a list of important tasks and prioritize them. Don't stress about the minor ones. Let them be and concentrate on what truly matters. Clean your house, garage, and any other disorganized areas.
- **Find a hobby.** A hobby can help you escape from life's pressures and relax. It allows you to focus your time and energy on something you enjoy. Participating in a hobby with others, such as friends or children, is even better.
- **Get enough sleep.** Aim for six to eight hours. If you can't get that amount, take naps during the day. Even "power naps"—15 to 30 minutes of rest where you close your eyes—help improve mental health.
- **Spend time with friends.** Friends have a way of making things seem better. They can help you get real and tell you when you're full of it. If you have the option to spend a night alone or with friends, choose to spend it with friends. If you don't have many friends, make some new ones.
- **Volunteer.** Helping others is a great way to boost your mental health by building self-worth.

Most importantly, get help if you need it! Don't let the stigma surrounding mental health prevent you from seeking help. Remember, seeking help is a sign of strength and that you're a 24:7 Dad.

Customizing the Habit

It's time to customize how you'll care for your mental health regularly. This decision involves reflecting on the following questions:

- What did I learn in this chapter that will help me take regular care of my mental health?
- How will I take care of my mental health regularly?

As with regular physical health care, customizing regular mental health care can involve any one or more of the seven options in Chapter 1 that works for you. If you're already doing things to care for your mental health that are working, keep doing them.

As you reflect on your customization, don't disregard ways of thinking. Those ways include the four tips you just learned for overall mental health, such as being patient. They also include things like being present in the moment, accepting others as they are and not trying to change them, and thinking through the consequences of actions before you take them. Men sometimes ignore ways of thinking because men tend to be action- and solutions-oriented. They like doing things that solve problems as quickly as possible. If they see a problem, they want to fix it. As a result, men can ignore adopting ways of thinking that affect their mental health, such as being grateful versus cynical.

As you customize this habit, consider not only ways of thinking and activities you'll start doing, but also ways of thinking and actions to stop that are or could potentially damage your mental health. Examples of ways of thinking to stop are the need to solve other people's problems, having unrealistic expectations for your co-parent's life or children's lives, and thinking you don't need time away from family to recharge mentally. Examples of actions to stop include using alcohol or overeating to reduce your stress, shutting others out when you need to grieve a loss, and repeatedly putting yourself in a situation that causes stress and could lead to depression, like a job that mentally drains you.

After you choose your methods for mental health care, compare them to your methods for physical health care. Are there overlapping methods? If so, that's fine because when you care for your mental health, it positively impacts your physical health and vice versa!

Deep-Dive Activity

A technique that can drive home the importance of self-care is to put yourself into the shoes of someone who deeply cares about you. This technique helps you empathize or connect with how another person thinks, feels, or views a situation.

Self-Care: Messages from Your Child

This activity helps you empathize with your children or another loved one in your life and their desire that you practice self-care.

1. Put yourself in the shoes of your child (or one of your children) or, if you don't have a child yet, of someone who loves or cares about you, such as your wife, partner, or best friend. If you chose a child, don't be concerned if your child isn't mature enough to give you those messages. The point is for you to see your self-care from another's perspective.

2. Acting as the person you chose, write three or four messages addressing ways that you could take better care of your

physical or mental health. For example, if you need to start going to a doctor or dentist for regular check-ups, write something like, "Dad, you need to begin seeing a dentist every six months." If seeing a counselor to discuss a toxic situation with your boss would help your mental health, write something like, "Dad, find a counselor who can help you work through the issues with your boss."

3. Set the messages aside for a day or two.
4. Review the messages and revise them if you want.
5. Review the messages with someone, such as the person you chose for this activity, a friend, or your accountability partner. Get their input and revise the messages if you want.
6. Take the next steps to follow through on the messages!

AI Prompts

Here are two hypothetical prompts I created for regular physical and mental health care. These are only examples of how AI can be helpful in identifying ways to apply both habits.

- **Physical health.** Acting as a recreation director at a summer camp, recommend two fun outdoor activities I can do with my five-year-old daughter. I can't run any longer because of a bad knee. Other than that restriction, we're not limited in the activities we can do.
- **Mental health.** I'm having difficulty establishing a weekly journaling schedule as a way to care for my mental health. I've tried journaling every Sunday, but I keep forgetting. Provide a sequence of steps for me to identify another approach.

For the physical healthcare habit, the AI I used recommended a nature scavenger hunt, outdoor story time, and a picnic. For the mental healthcare habit, it suggested a five-step approach to establishing a weekly journaling schedule that involves why I'm forgetting, reviewing my current routine and habits, brainstorming alternative times to journal, experimenting with new methods, and evaluating and adjusting. Interestingly, it advised that while reviewing my habits, I should look for a habit I could "piggyback" journaling on ... habit stacking!

Chapter 4

Fathering Skills: Holistic Fathering & Modeling Healthy Masculinity

"Try not to become a man of success but rather try to become a man of value."

—Albert Einstein, physicist

John Mugabi was a Ugandan boxer who competed professionally in the 1980s and 1990s. As one of the best super-welterweights of his time, he earned the nickname "The Beast" due to his raw power. He quickly rose in the rankings, winning every match by knockout until he moved up to the middleweight class to fight "Marvelous" Marvin Hagler, where he lost.

What does John "The Beast" Mugabi have to do with fathering? I'm getting to that.

My younger daughter, Jillian, was a challenging toddler. A perfect infant, she gave my wife and me a front-row seat to the "terrible twos." She began throwing tantrums, became defiant, and tested our patience to its limits. She was unusually strong for her age. Muscular and built like a gymnast, she became difficult to keep up with once she became mobile. She was observant, quiet, and always on the move. Like a stealth fighter, she flew under our radar. We often wondered where she was, only to find her climbing on a chair, table, or kitchen counter.

Jillian's energy matched her strength. To help dissipate that energy, I created a game called "Attack Baby." I encouraged her to run at me, trying to take me down. Sometimes, I'd lie on the ground. When she reached me, I'd pick her up and roll her away. She would come at me again and again.

Because she was strong and muscular, I gave her the nickname Jillian "The Beast" Mugabi. (She would laugh every time I said it.) Sometimes, Jillian became so excited that she pounded me with her fists or kicked me. She could hit me with enough force that it hurt. When she did that, I stopped the game. I was teaching her how to control her emotions with my displeasure and signaling when she had gone too far.

We played that game for several years. Jillian still remembers it fondly to this day.

The two habits you'll learn to apply in this chapter will help you leverage the skills of the 24:7 Dad that provide the holistic involvement and the healthy masculine model your children need. In doing so, you'll learn what fathering is, how it has evolved, and the elements of the foundation for being a good co-parent. You'll also continue to learn how the model of masculinity you subscribe to affects your fathering and about two pain points that affect a father's ability to provide a healthy masculine model for his children: struggling with intimacy and sexuality. Prepare to be challenged at a deeper level than you may be used to.

Trait: Fathering Skills

The 24:7 Dad understands and embraces his vital role as a parent and model for his children. He actively participates in everyday moments—morning routines, school events, extracurricular activities, homework sessions, and bedtime rituals. The 24:7 Dad knows effective parenting means leveraging the distinct strengths that he and his co-parent bring to raising their children.

Embracing the role of the 24:7 Dad involves committing to the holistic involvement that your children need. Holistic involvement means that you're more than a physically present father. You're also fully committed to your children by being present emotionally, intellectually, and spiritually. This chapter is about achieving that level of involvement by establishing two habits: holistic fathering and modeling healthy masculinity.

Habit: Holistic Fathering

Being a father is a role similar to being a brother, friend, husband, or employee. Roles come with specific responsibilities or duties. Unless you're a single father raising his children alone, you'll carry out a holistic fathering role in conjunction with the family role your co-parent plays. You need to decide how that role will help you to be as holistically involved as possible.

To start down this decision-making path, it's important to reflect on the factors that have or will influence your fathering. You learned in the Introduction that there are many individual, relational, and systemic (or cultural) factors. The relational factor that affects fathers most deeply is what they learned about fathering from their own father. Even a physically or emotionally absent father like mine teaches a son something about being a father, even if that's the limited but powerful lesson that a father isn't involved.

Because the relational factor is such a crucial influence on fathering, an important part of your journey to become a 24:7 Dad involves exploring how your upbringing contributes to the father you are or will become. Complete the following statements as you consider how your experiences as a child reflect your approach to fathering.

If this is the first time you've explored this influence, it might put you in touch with something uncomfortable or painful. If so, talk with your accountability partner, someone you trust, or a professional counselor to help you process it.

- I'm like my father (or the man who raised me) in the following ways:

  _____.

- I'm not like my father (or the man who raised me) in the following ways:

  _____.

Your responses provide a sense of how much your fathering role is or could be similar or different from your father's. It also provides a window into how involved your father (or father figure) was from a holistic perspective. How did your responses reflect any one or more aspects of physical, emotional, intellectual, or spiritual involvement?

Let's continue exploring how you're similar or different from your father by completing four additional statements that will identify more specifically how similar or different you are. This will give you a more complete picture of how he influenced your fathering based on the role he played in your family growing up.

- My father's (or the man who raised me) main role in the family was

  _____.

- Other parts of his (or the man's who raised me) role included

  _____.

- What I like about how my father (or the man who raised me) fulfilled his role was
  _____.

- What I don't like about how my father (or the man who raised me) fulfilled his role was
  _____.

Reflecting on your role, how is it similar or different from your father's? Why are you fulfilling a similar or different role? Did you make a conscious decision to have a similar or dissimilar one?

Like me, some fathers make a conscious decision to follow in their father's footsteps or not due to the impact a good or poor father had on them. Other fathers simply fall into a role that's like or unlike their father's, unaware of his influence until completing statements like these. Regardless of whether or not you decided to follow in your father's footsteps, if you like how he fulfilled his role it could explain why you have a similar role. Not liking how he fulfilled his role could explain why your role is different.

The Father's Evolving Role

Next to the influence of a father's upbringing, the cultural environment in which men grow up and become a father has been the second most powerful factor influencing the holistic fathering role. In the past, the cultural environment has dictated the responsibilities associated with the roles parents assume. But the influence of that environment on the division of those responsibilities has lessened in recent decades as parents increasingly customize them to fit their own circumstances. Today's American fathers and mothers often divide their responsibilities differently than in previous generations. These parents decide who does what based on personal preferences and skills rather than what family tradition, culture, or religion dictates, especially when it comes to gender-based roles—namely, the emphasis on fathers providing financially and mothers taking care of children and performing domestic work. That evolution has occurred in most other Western countries, with many Eastern countries evolving at a similar pace or close behind.[1,2]

> **Sticking with Tradition**
>
> *Despite the evolving roles of fathers and mothers, many couples choose a traditional gender-based division of responsibilities. This choice can be influenced by personal preference, culture, or religion. It may also be shaped by family tradition, with parents following in their own parents' footsteps. The most important factor in deciding how to divide responsibilities is parents contributing equally to the decision-making process and being satisfied with the outcome. Parents should remain flexible in adjusting their responsibilities as circumstances change.*

This evolution has led most fathers to spend more time with their children. Sociologist Wendy Wang, director of research at the Institute for Family Studies, analyzed data from the U.S. Census Bureau comparing the time resident fathers spent with their children in the past two decades (2003 compared to 2021–2022). She found that while

---

[1] Novianti, R., Suarman, & Islami, N. (2023). Parenting in cultural perspective: A systematic review of paternal role across cultures. *Journal of Ethnic and Cultural Studies, 10*(1), 22–44.

[2] Praphat, R., & Theurer, J. A. (2019). An exploratory cross-cultural study: Fathers' early involvement with infants. *Early Child Development and Care, 191*(11), 1832–1845.

the amount of time American fathers spent with their children rose by more than one hour per week overall, it increased more for some types of fathers than others. Married and cohabiting fathers spent more time with their children, while single fathers spent the same amount of time. Specifically, the time of married fathers rose from 6.8 hours per week to 8.0 hours, the time of cohabiting fathers rose from 5.1 hours per week to 6.7 hours, and the time of single fathers rose only from 6.2 hours per week to 6.3 hours.[3]

This evolution has also influenced time dedicated to childcare and housework, two traditional responsibilities of mothers. Researchers at the Pew Research Center analyzed data on the amount of time parents spend on these responsibilities over a recent 45-year period (1965–2011). They found that the proportion of time fathers dedicated to childcare and housework increased from 14 percent to 31 percent, while mothers' proportion decreased from 81 percent to 59 percent. Fathers spent twice as much time on housework, whereas mothers halved their housework. Fathers also tripled time spent with their children.[4] A key factor influencing this evolution is economic changes that have created more dual-earner families. As more women and mothers worked outside the home, it put pressure on fathers to step up and broaden their role, and they have. But something more profoundly cultural is also at play.

---

[3]Wang, W. (2023, October 24). *American dads are more involved than ever—especially college-educated or married dads.* Institute for Family Studies. https://ifstudies.org/blog/american-dads-are-more-involved-than-everespecially-college-educated-or-married-dads

[4]Pew Research Center. (2013, March 14). *Modern parenthood: Roles of moms and dads converge as they balance work and family.* Pew Research Center. https://www.pewresearch.org/social-trends/2013/03/14/modern-parenthood-roles-of-moms-and-dads-converge-as-they-balance-work-and-family/

As you learned in the Introduction, today's fathers view their role as more central to their personal identity compared to previous generations. In other words, the model for what it means to be a good father has changed. Today's fathers have a stronger internal drive to be fathers who are holistically involved. Researchers refer to this as "intrinsic motivation," which is crucial for becoming a 24:7 Dad. This type of motivation arises from within rather than from an external influence (extrinsic). While extrinsic motivation can initially be effective in prompting fathers to explore becoming a better father, it tends to be a less stable motivator over time. One reason National Fatherhood Initiative® (NFI) programs transform fathers who initially enroll due to an extrinsic motivator—such as court orders—is that their motivation shifts within the first few weeks of the program. Once they realize how much the program will help them, extrinsic motivation gives way to intrinsic motivation. That intrinsic motivation helps them become more holistically involved fathers. When asked about the most significant impact of NFI programs, fathers often point to the moment their intrinsic motivation kicked in: when they realized that being an involved father means more than being only a financial provider.

Fathers' Natural Strengths

Now that you understand the holistic role of the 24:7 Dad, it's time to explore the skills required to execute that role. *Fathering is a set of skills you can learn to master.* It's no different from your other roles. If you want to be an outstanding manager at work, for example, you need a specific skill set to execute that job effectively. Becoming a 24:7 Dad involves recognizing the skills necessary to succeed in a holistic role, improving the skills you already excel at, and developing and honing the ones you don't excel at.

To explore these skills, it helps to understand what research shows about fathers' natural strengths in holistic involvement. For example, when it comes to parent–child play, fathers are generally more physical with their children. While mothers use toys and other items to engage their children, fathers are often the toy themselves. Children like crawling, hanging, and riding on their fathers. Fathers tend to push their children to explore their environment more than mothers do, often standing farther away while mothers remain closer. Fathers are more likely to guide and challenge their children rather than simply assist them. Fathers also hold their children differently, often facing outward. Those fathering behaviors benefit children in specific ways, including overall brain development, learning to regulate their emotions, improving their balance (sense of equilibrium), and appropriate risk-taking.[5] The ways in which fathers and mothers read to their children also differ. Fathers ask their children more open-ended questions, challenging the children's thinking and expanding their language. They also engage in more complex conversations and parent–child "interlocking contact" (mutual touching).[6] These differences are key reasons why fathers benefit children in ways mothers don't. It's also why fathering is distinct from mothering, and fathering skills and parenting skills are distinct traits of the 24:7 Dad.

Exploring the skills necessary to carry out a holistic role is also aided by knowing you may have specific preferences for how you'll

---

[5]Pruett, K. D. (2000). *Fatherneed: Why father care is as essential as mother care for your child*. Free Press.

[6]Cutler, L., & Palkovitz, R. (2023, April). *Reading with dad – influences on fathers' engagement in shared book reading and why it matters for children's development*. Child and Family Blog. https://childandfamilyblog.com/reading-with-dad/

execute that role. As you learned earlier in this chapter, many parents decide the roles they'll play based on personal preferences. Those preferences may or may not be the same as most fathers. For example, a study of 436 adults raising children with a partner found that men preferred home maintenance and yard care and wanted primary responsibility for those tasks more than women did. Although there were some household tasks that men enjoyed much more than women, and some household and childcare tasks that women preferred much more than men, there wasn't one childcare task that men liked more than women.[7]

Getting in touch with preferences for your holistic role will make it easier to fulfill it. At the same time, you may assume a responsibility you don't prefer because you excel at it, and your co-parent doesn't. The bottom line is that you're a unique individual and father (or father-to-be), and that's why this book helps you customize your approach to fathering. The questions in the Customizing the Habit section below will help you identify your preferences.

Being a Good Co-Parent

Return to the statements you completed earlier in this chapter. Is there any part of your fathering role related to being a good husband or partner in raising your children? If there is, congratulations. Many fathers in NFI programs don't initially recognize the importance that being a good co-parent plays in raising healthy children. It's easier to be a good father if you're a good co-parent. Additionally, how you interact with your co-parent—how you treat them as an individual

---

[7]Bleske-Rechek, A., & Gunseor, M. M. (2022). Gendered perspectives on sharing the load: Men's and women's attitudes toward family roles and household and childcare tasks. *Evolutionary Behavioral Sciences, 16*(3), 201–219.

and in working together as a parenting team—will greatly influence your children's relationships. For example, treating your co-parent with respect and choosing how to work with your co-parent to carry out your respective responsibilities in raising your children sets a powerful example for your children. We'll discuss the overall relationship with your co-parent in the next chapter as part of the creating a loving co-parenting relationship habit.

No matter how you completed the statements earlier in this chapter, your responses reflect a simple fact: parents divide the responsibilities of family life. One of the things I'm most proud of is how well my wife Kayla and I co-parented our daughters. Many of our responsibilities overlapped. For example, we both worked outside the home, cooked, and performed housework. I managed our finances, took care of the yard, and coordinated our daughters' sports activities. My wife managed our religious and social lives as well as our daughters' school activities. While our need for two incomes required that we share many responsibilities, we divided them based on what we excelled at together and alone. It was a conscious choice based on our preferences and respective skill sets.

Effective co-parenting depends on practical skills—like listening and communicating clearly, which you'll learn in the next chapter—and fundamental attitudes like respect and flexibility. The stronger your foundation of mutual respect and willingness to negotiate, the more effectively you can apply those co-parenting skills. To evaluate your current foundation, complete the "Effective Co-Parenting Foundation Checklist" below.

Effective Co-Parenting Foundation Checklist

Place a checkmark in the box if you agree with the statement about yourself as a co-parent. When responding, reflect on the responsibilities you and your co-parent ("their" and "them" in the statements) have in raising your children. It can be helpful to put yourself in your co-parent's shoes and answer as they would about you. If you don't have children yet, reflect on ways that you currently support your partner or past partners in general.

1. I listen to their point of view. ☐
2. I respect their point of view. ☐
3. I don't violate their boundaries. ☐
4. I clearly communicate my point of view to them. ☐
5. I share my boundaries with them. ☐
6. I negotiate with them when we have different opinions. ☐
7. I share my thoughts and feelings with them calmly. ☐
8. I'm willing to accept that their opinion may be better than mine. ☐
9. I support a shared decision, even when I don't agree with it. ☐
10. I can let go of control and allow them to make the decision. ☐
11. I'm willing to walk away when a discussion gets too heated so that we can revisit a decision later on when we've both calmed down. ☐

The statements you didn't agree with reflect areas of growth in building a foundation for effective co-parenting. Don't worry if you didn't agree with most of the statements. Many fathers struggle with adopting the traits in the checklist, especially fathers whose relationship with their co-parent has a troubling history that makes it difficult to co-parent effectively. Many of the fathers starting NFI's programs have a poor relationship with their co-parent. But in laying the foundation for effective co-parenting, they turn that relationship into an amicable or even good one by the program's conclusion. They're willing to take the first step for the benefit of their children. If you have a poor relationship with your co-parent, have the courage to take that step.

Quick Win: Using Humor

Most of what you've learned so far about applying the 12 habits is serious. Fortunately, being a 24:7 Dad isn't just about serious matters. Your ability to bring lighter skills into your fathering is key to being a 24:7 Dad. A quick win in applying a holistic fathering role is using humor with your children. Research shows that using humor has long-term benefits for fathers' relationships with their children. For example, a study of 312 adults found that those whose own parents used humor to raise them were more likely to have a more positive relationship as adults with their parents than did those adults whose parents didn't use humor.[8]

If you're a naturally funny person, using humor will come easily. If you don't use humor often in your relationships, don't hesitate to create a plan for using it in ways that are age-appropriate for your children, such as making funny faces and noises with a toddler. Identify specific actions, such as learning some jokes with a child in middle school, and when you'll use them. But I want to share a word of caution. It's possible to use humor in ways that can harm children and others. Harmful humor makes light of something someone says or does, such as mispronouncing a word or tripping and falling. It can involve actions or words that hurt someone's body or emotions, such as when a parent won't stop tickling their child after the child asks them to stop, or when a parent pushes their child into a pool against the child's wishes.

---

[8]Emery, L., Libera, A., Lehman, E., & Levi, B. H. (2024). Humor in parenting: Does it have a role? *PLOS ONE, 19*(7), e0306311.

Customizing the Habit

It's time to customize your holistic fathering role. Unlike the previous habits that involved reflecting on only one question, customizing this habit involves reflecting on many questions:

- What have I learned so far in this chapter that will help me with holistic fathering?
- Based on the fathering model I had growing up, what will I apply in my fathering?
- Based on the fathering model I had growing up, what won't I apply in my fathering?
- What are the skills I excel at and use (or plan to use) in raising my children?
- How do those skills touch on each element of holistic involvement (physical, emotional, intellectual, and spiritual)?
- What skills don't I excel at and need to work on to be a more holistically involved father?
- How do those skills touch on each element of holistic involvement (physical, emotional, intellectual, and spiritual)?
- What parts of the foundation for being a good co-parent do I already possess?
- What parts of the foundation do I need to put into place to be a good co-parent?

As you can see, there's a lot to consider in customizing this habit! Take your time in reflecting on each question because it will be well worth it. Customizing holistic involvement can involve any one or more of the seven customization options in Chapter 1 that work for you. If you're already doing things that involve you holistically, keep doing them. Remember to consider habit stacking.

Habit: Modeling Healthy Masculinity

You learned in Chapter 3 about models of masculinity that instruct many boys and men to deny physical pain and suppress emotions. Those models have many other instructions, such as how to treat women or the professions that are acceptable for men to pursue. Some of those instructions are healthy and others unhealthy for men, women, children, families, and communities. You'll learn more about some of the unhealthy instructions later in the discussion of intimacy and sexuality, two common pain points in modeling healthy masculinity.

To start our discussion of this habit and how influential models of masculinity are in shaping the attitudes, beliefs, and behavior of fathers, I'll have you complete some statements that—surprise, surprise—will raise your awareness about the most influential person in most father's lives in the transmission of the model's instructions: their own father. As you consider your responses, remember that what your father did—his actions or behaviors—were instructions as influential as what he said to you.

- The main instruction my father (or the man who raised me) sent about being a man was
  _____.

- What I liked about that instruction was
  _____.

- What I disliked about that instruction was
  _____.

- The effect of that instruction on the man I became was
  _____.

- The effect that instruction had on the father I became (or will become) is
  _____.

Completing these statements about the instructions can help you see the link between what fathers learn about being a man and how what they learn affects their fathering. For example, if you learned that being an acceptable man means you don't seek help for mental health issues, you'll be reluctant to talk with your child who is facing a mental health crisis, especially if that child is a son who you expect should "suck it up." With that example in mind, do your responses identify that link? If so, how?

Cross-Cultural Masculinity Traits

You also learned in Chapter 3 that the model of masculinity you possess transmits instructions of the acceptable and desirable traits that men should possess. This collection of traits represents "Dad Perfect." You value these traits because your culture values them. Even though the traits you value might differ from a friend's who was raised in a different culture, there are traits of different cultural models that overlap, making them cross-cultural.[9,10] These traits include:

- Ambition
- Assertiveness
- Competitiveness
- Confidence
- Courage

---

[9]Worthy, L. D., Lavigne, T., & Romero, F. (2020). *Culture and psychology: How people shape and are shaped by culture*. Glendale Community College.
[10]Wong, Y. J., Ho, M.-H. R., Wang, S.-Y., & Miller, I. S. K. (2017). Meta-analyses of the relationship between conformity to masculine norms and mental health-related outcomes. *Journal of Counseling Psychology, 64*(6), 805–823.

- Being honorable
- Being in control (emotionally)
- Exerting power
- Being respectful
- Taking risks
- Achieving success (financially/materially)

Men learn these traits from cultural institutions, with family being the most influential institution. The other institutions include mass and social media, entertainment, religion, education, government, and civic organizations. These are powerful models because their instructions are everywhere! You can't escape them. Their power explains why it's so difficult for boys and men who don't adhere to the model's traits. Step out of line, and you're called out for being different, odd, or weird.

The cross-cultural traits aren't inherently good or bad. It's the messages a culture conveys about how to express them that can be healthy or unhealthy. For instance, exerting power is often portrayed as physical or emotional control over others (dominance) instead of as empowering others to retain control over their choices. Taking risks can come across as reckless behavior that endangers oneself and others, rather than as the initiative to start a business that provides a product or service that enhances lives. Achieving success is expressed in obtaining financial wealth at the expense of others or the environment, rather than obtaining financial wealth used to start a grant-making foundation that funds projects aimed at reducing poverty.

As the diagram below shows, cultural institutions filter the traits into specific instructions that guide the behavior of boys and men.

MODEL OF MASCULINITY

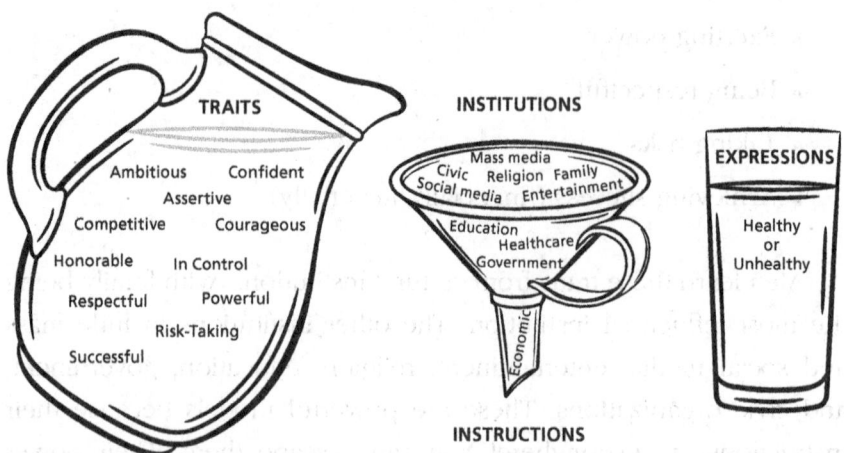

Research underscores how devastating these unhealthy expressions can be for men. These expressions not only negatively impact men's health generally and prevent men from seeking the help they need, but they also increase the risk of suicide.[11] Fortunately, cultural models of masculinity, their traits, and the instructions about how to express them are evolving to embrace new traits and healthier expressions. They're also becoming more cross-cultural.[12,13] Models have

---

[11]Galvez-Sánchez, C. M., Camacho-Ruiz, J. A., Castelli, L., & Limiñana-Gras, R. M. (2025). Exploring the role of masculinity in male suicide: A systematic review. *Psychiatry International*, *6*(1), 2.

[12]Hassan, M. (2025). Masculinity in flux: Media representations and the shaping of gender norms across cultural contexts. *International Journal of Research and Innovation in Social Science*, *9*(2), 2400–2404.

[13]Zubiri-Esnaola, H., Gutiérrez-Fernández, N., & Guo, M. (2021). "No more insecurities": New alternative masculinities' communicative acts generate desire and equality to obliterate offensive sexual statements. *Frontiers in Psychology*, *12*, 674186.

incorporated new traits like nurturing, emotional expressiveness, empathy, and vulnerability and are prioritizing work–family balance more than ever.[14] That's great news for fathers. For example, fathers who embrace nurturing are more sensitive, positive, and more attached to their infants.[15] They're also better co-parents.[16] These evolving models help explain why many fathers today feel more comfortable seeking help for their physical and mental health issues.[17]

As a result, many fathers are reframing two pain points that have been hard for men to explore and discuss: intimacy and sexuality. These expressions of human nature are heavily influenced by cultural models of masculinity. Understanding the roles they play in fathering and expressing them in healthy ways is essential to being a 24:7 Dad.

Intimacy

Because people can attach different meanings to the word "intimacy," I want you to write down the first few words or phrases that come to mind when you read that word.

---

[14]Harrington, B., Van Deusen, F., & Humberd, B. (2011). *The new dad: Caring, committed, and conflicted.* Boston College Center for Work and Family.

[15]Schoppe-Sullivan, S. J., Shafer, K., Olofson, E., & Kamp Dush, C. M. (2021). Fathers' parenting and coparenting behavior in dual-earner families: Contributions of traditional masculinity, father nurturing role beliefs, and maternal gate closing. *Psychology of Men & Masculinities, 22*(3), 538–550.

[16]Kuo, P. X., Volling, B. L., & Gonzalez, R. (2017). His, hers, or theirs? Coparenting after the birth of a second child. *Journal of Family Psychology, 31*(6), 710–720.

[17]Guinness, D. (2024, October 2). *Sex, self-worth and stigma: The links between men's wellbeing and attitudes towards sex.* Beyond Equality. https://www.beyondequality.org/blog-posts/sex-self-worth-and-stigma-the-links-between-mens-wellbeing-and-attitudes-towards-sex

Did you write down words or phrases like "a close friend," "personal," "confidential," or "emotional?" Or did you write down words or phrases like "sex," "sexual," or "making love?" Is your list short or long? Do the items in your list address emotional and physical forms of intimacy?

Your answer to the last question is the most important one of those for understanding intimacy's meaning. Intimacy is the ability to feel close to another person emotionally or physically. The desire and need for emotional and physical intimacy are parts of human nature, and they're critical to survival. This need existed from the moment you were born. You needed the emotional presence and physical touch of your parents and other caregivers to start on a healthy developmental journey.

That journey includes learning how to be emotionally and physically intimate with others in healthy ways. Unfortunately, many men don't learn this skill, especially if they're neglected, abused physically or emotionally, or abandoned by their parents. Many men struggle with healthy expressions of emotional and physical intimacy, which becomes a pain point when they become a father. They're socialized to value physical intimacy and devalue emotional intimacy. Moreover, they learn that the only way to be physically intimate is by having sex. Many boys mark their passage from boyhood to manhood with their first sexual encounter and tie their self-worth to the number of their sexual encounters.

Many men learn to devalue emotional intimacy to the point they avoid it, especially with other men, even though being emotionally intimate with other men is essential to men's overall well-being. As a result of avoiding emotional intimacy (with women or men), it's difficult for these men to develop the emotional intimacy required for healthy, long-lasting romantic relationships and friendships. They often don't know how to be emotionally intimate or understand, ironically, how emotional intimacy enhances the sexual form of physical intimacy they've learned to value.

This difficulty in expressing emotional intimacy can lead to problems in romantic relationships because women often seek more than sexual intimacy. Women sometimes use derogatory terms, such as "shallow" and "tool," to describe men who see sex as the only form of physical intimacy. These men flee when relationships progress beyond the infatuation phase and into their natural ebbs and flows. Like a dragonfly darting from one reed to another in a marsh, they move rapidly from one romantic relationship to another, never staying grounded long enough in any one of them to experience a more meaningful relationship.

Not all men devalue emotional intimacy. However, because many men learn to connect emotional intimacy with sexual intimacy, they only feel comfortable being emotionally intimate when they're in a romantic relationship. As a result, they put a great deal of pressure on their partners to be the sole source for their emotional intimacy. More than 50 studies on intimacy found that this pressure leads men to place more importance on the emotional and physical benefits they derive from romantic relationships than women do. As a result, men experience greater emotional pain from breakups.[18]

I wouldn't be surprised if you're wondering how men with this view of intimacy ever stay in romantic relationships long enough to become fathers! Aside from men who become fathers unintentionally through brief sexual encounters or short-term relationships, most men plan to become fathers in long-term relationships, typically after marriage. But for a man struggling with healthy expressions of emotional and physical intimacy, it doesn't matter when or how he becomes a father. He'll not only struggle with having a healthy relationship with

---

[18]Wahring, I. V., Simpson, J A., & Van Lange, P. A. M. (2024). Romantic relationships matter more to men than to women. *Behavioral and Brain Sciences*, 1–64.

his partner, but he'll also struggle with providing his children the holistically involved father they need. This struggle makes it easier for some fathers to abandon their families, perpetuating a cycle that harms their children and risks the well-being of future generations.

If you've struggled with physical and emotional intimacy, the good news is that the guidance, tips, and skills throughout this book will help! For example, developing a relationship with an accountability partner is a great step toward comfort with emotional intimacy because it requires being vulnerable. Caring for your physical and mental health will help your body and mind to be more receptive to giving, receiving, and enjoying healthy expressions of emotional and physical intimacy. The communication skills you'll learn later will help you to be more comfortable expressing your desire for intimacy with romantic partners, friends, and family members.

Emotional Intimacy with Other Men

If you want to become more comfortable with emotional intimacy, you must be willing to be emotionally intimate with other men and fathers. The best way to do that is by being vulnerable. It's not easy. A survey conducted by the Survey Center on American Life found that only 30 percent of men—whether young or old—turned to friends for emotional support, compared to 48 percent of women.[19] As a result, many men feel uncomfortable sharing their struggles in fathering with other men. A primary reason is that men lack emotionally safe spaces to be vulnerable in front of other men. You must be intentional in creating or seeking out these spaces. Once established, you can signal to other men that there's a safe place to bear one's soul.

---

[19]Survey Center on American Life. (2021, June). *The state of American friendship: Change, challenges, and loss.* https://www.americansurveycenter.org/research/the-state-of-american-friendship-change-challenges-and-loss/

Creating or seeking a safe place is well worth it. I've seen the power of these places in transforming men by giving them permission to be vulnerable. NFI's programs are often implemented with small groups of fathers. These groups provide a safe space for being vulnerable with other fathers who face the same challenges. For many fathers, this is the first time in their lives they've entered such a space, including in prisons and other correctional facilities, where being vulnerable is especially challenging because it can signal weakness and invite abuse. Even in these settings, fathers can transform into better fathers when they have permission from other fathers to be vulnerable. An evaluation of InsideOut Dad®, NFI's program for incarcerated fathers that's run with small groups, found that sharing vulnerability improves these fathers' overall emotional well-being.[20]

Sexuality

Because fathers can struggle with intimacy, they can also struggle with a related part of human nature: sexuality. Before continuing to read, reflect on the meaning of sexuality. Write down your thoughts.

I'll wager that "sex" or "having sex" came to mind, just as they might have when you reflected on intimacy's meaning. That's fine unless that's all you thought about. Many men don't know the difference between sex and sexuality. Sexuality encompasses aspects of human nature like intimacy. Having sex (or the desire for it) is only one part of our sexuality. To nurture their sexuality, men must learn about its facets. In addition to intimacy, those facets include body image, touch, and physical sexual response.

---

[20]Turner, J. J., Bradford, K., Higginbotham, B. J., & Coppin, A. (2021). Examining the outcomes of the InsideOut Dad fatherhood education program for incarcerated minority fathers. *The Family Journal, 29*(3), 305–315.

Many men don't understand that as a part of human nature the healthy expression of sexuality is crucial to their physical and emotional health. They don't recognize the importance of healthy sexuality and instead focus on having sex as the be-all and end-all of their sexual nature. Equating sex with sexuality leads many men away from the idea that they must care for their sexuality.

Understanding your sexuality and its healthy expression is essential for maintaining healthy sexual relationships with your co-parent or other romantic partner. This understanding and expression promote sexually responsible behavior—a desire to not violate another person sexually and protect yourself against being sexually violated. Responsible sexual behavior helps build mutual respect and trust within romantic relationships. And when the time comes to help your children understand what it means to have a healthy romantic relationship, understanding your sexuality and its healthy expression will play a crucial role.

Your sexuality is affected by your "sexual self-worth." Self-worth is the overall thoughts (self-concept) and feelings (self-esteem) you have about yourself as a sexual being. In addition to sexuality and the factors that comprise it, other aspects of sexual self-worth include:

- Your physical ability to have sex
- Respect for your partner's willingness to engage in sex and their desire for specific sexual acts
- The level of trust you place in your partner in sharing physical and emotional intimacy
- Your level of responsibility for the consequences of having sex, such as unplanned pregnancies and contracting or spreading sexually transmitted infections

Becoming a 24:7 Dad involves striving to have a high level of sexual self-worth. To determine your level of sexual self-worth, complete the survey below.

Sexual Self-Worth Survey

Place a checkmark next to your degree of comfort with each of the 10 parts of sexual self-worth. After you rate each one, convert your ratings to a numerical score as follows: Low = 1; Average = 2; and High = 3. The total score indicates your overall level of sexual self-worth.

1. Body image ☐ Low ☐ Average ☐ High
2. Physically able to have sex ☐ Low ☐ Average ☐ High
3. Ability to feel physically intimate ☐ Low ☐ Average ☐ High
4. Ability to feel emotionally intimate ☐ Low ☐ Average ☐ High
5. Ability to become sexually aroused ☐ Low ☐ Average ☐ High
6. Being responsible sexually ☐ Low ☐ Average ☐ High
7. Being respectful sexually ☐ Low ☐ Average ☐ High
8. Ability to trust another sexually ☐ Low ☐ Average ☐ High
9. Overall ability to protect your sexuality ☐ Low ☐ Average ☐ High
10. Overall ability to protect your partner's sexuality ☐ Low ☐ Average ☐ High

Total Score = _____ (0–10 is low sexual self-worth, 11–20 is average or moderate sexual self-worth, and 21–30 is high sexual self-worth)

Before you continue reading, set aside your score and reflect on how easy or difficult it was to rate your sexual self-worth. Write down your thoughts.

If it was easy to rate your sexual self-worth, you're probably more open to exploring this aspect of yourself than someone who found rating their sexual self-worth difficult or even skipped doing it. If you have low or moderate self-worth, that openness is crucial for improving your sexual self-worth. If you have high sexual self-worth, that openness is crucial for maintaining it.

Quick Win: Talk to Your Children About Body Image

You learned earlier in this chapter that your children need you to be emotionally and physically intimate with them in healthy ways. One reason is the importance of helping your children with developing a positive body image, which refers to the thoughts and feelings they have about their bodies. You can have a positive image, a negative image, or something in between.

A quick win in modeling healthy masculinity is discussing body image with your children. This discussion is powerful because it shows your children a healthy expression of emotional intimacy. This discussion is also powerful because a negative body image sets the stage for anxiety and depression, which can lead to children harming themselves, such as by self-cutting and developing eating disorders. We'll get to the "how" of having this discussion shortly, but first I want to talk about the cultural messages sent to boys and girls about their bodies. Being aware of these messages will help you in discussing body image with a son or daughter.

You're probably aware of the struggle that many girls and women have with a negative body image. Expressions of their struggle are prevalent in the media, and there are programs that help females explore their body image and develop ways to improve it. What people are much less aware of is how many boys and men have a negative body image as well.[21] This lack of awareness means that there is almost no mention of males struggling with body image, and only a few resources to help them improve it.

What causes females and males to develop a negative body image are unrealistic images of what a female and male should strive to look like. These messages implant an image of a person chiseled out of stone—a slim and fit model for females and a muscular and fit model for males. However, females receive these messages much more often and from many more sources, making it harder to avoid the messages' negative impact on their self-worth. Males are also given more leeway to look different from the ideal.

With that knowledge in place, here are some tips for discussing this topic with your children:

- **Get in touch with your own body image.** If you haven't reflected on your own body image, it can prevent you from having a discussion with your children about theirs. If you have a negative body image, it doesn't mean you shouldn't discuss body image with your children, but you should at least be addressing it. Speak with a trained professional in this area if you need to.

- **Be a good role model by caring for your body.** Explain how caring for their body helps your children develop a positive body image. If you don't care for your body, such as with exercise, proper nutrition, and skin care, your children will notice the hypocrisy when you tell them to care for theirs.

---

[21] Alcaraz-Ibáñez, M., Sicilia, Á., & Paterna, A. (2020). Associations between body dissatisfaction and self-reported anxiety and depression in otherwise healthy men: A systematic review and meta-analysis. *PLOS ONE, 15*(2), e0229268.

- **Use positive language.** Avoid discussing your children's and others' physical appearances. Instead, focus on their positive, healthy traits and the benefits of caring for their bodies, such as strength and stamina.

- **Discuss media messages.** Raise your children's awareness about the harmful messages that both mass and social media send about body image, such as the constant focus on how people look. When your children ask about physical appearance, help them recognize that many body types can be fit and attractive. Share examples of fit, beautiful people with different body types.

- **Limit social media usage.** Harmful, shallow messages about body image are widespread on social media. Children can be ruthless and shaming toward one another about physical appearance.

- **Encourage healthy friendships.** Help your children spend time with friends who have a positive body image and accept them regardless of their physical appearance.

- **Encourage healthy eating and physical activity habits.** These are essential because you want your children to care for their bodies rather than neglect them. This tip involves not only what they do with and put into their bodies but also what they put on their bodies and how they protect it, such as moisturizer and sunscreen. Apply what you've learned about forming habits in this book to support your children in eating healthily and exercising regularly.

- **When your children go through puberty, discuss its effects on the body and mind.** The effects on their body, like acne and weight gain, can embarrass children and provide other children with a reason to ridicule them. Explain that these effects are normal and that it might take their bodies time to adjust to the changes.[22] But if you or your child become concerned about a change in their body, seek medical guidance.

Discussing body image with your children can be uncomfortable. To prepare for a discussion, talk with your co-parent (or another person you trust) and get their input. It might be helpful to have your co-parent join the discussion, especially if their participation will increase your comfort in addressing this important issue.

Customizing the Habit

It's time to customize how you'll model healthy masculinity. As with customizing holistic fathering, deciding how you'll customize this habit involves reflecting on many questions:

- What have I learned in this chapter that will help me model healthy masculinity?
- Which traits of masculinity have I learned that serve me well in my fathering, or will serve me well when I become a father?
- How can I continue leveraging them?
- Which traits of masculinity have I learned that don't serve me well in my fathering, or won't serve me well when I become a father?
- How can I overcome those?
- How will I model masculinity for my children in ways that will help and not harm them?

---

[22]Ulrich, S., & Paulson, D. (2021, August 9). *Promoting healthy body image in children, teens*. Mayo Clinic Health System. https://www.mayocliniche althsystem.org/hometown-health/speaking-of-health/promoting-healthy-body-image-in-children-teens

- Do I need to become more comfortable with discussing or expressing emotional intimacy?
- If I do, how will I become more comfortable with discussing or expressing it?
- Do I need to become more comfortable with discussing or expressing physical intimacy in non-sexual ways?
- If I do, how will I become more comfortable with discussing or expressing it?
- Do I need to raise my level of sexual self-worth?
- If I do, how will I raise it?
- Am I protecting my sexual self-worth from violation by others?
- If no, how will I better protect it?
- Am I respectful of my romantic partner's sexual self-worth?
- If no, how will I become more respectful of it?

These questions can be difficult to answer because they require being vulnerable and a deep level of reflection that many men haven't experienced. Don't worry if you can't answer them all. Talking with your accountability partner or a professional counselor could be helpful.

As with applying and customizing the previous habits, modeling healthy masculinity can involve any one or more of the seven customization options in Chapter 1 that work for you. If you're already doing things that model healthy masculinity, keep doing them. How can you incorporate habit stacking?

Deep-Dive Activity

The activity below will help you model healthy masculinity for your children.

Fathering Skills: Becoming a Better Man

Use this activity to identify and prioritize the traits of healthy masculinity you want to further develop and model for your children.

1. List the top 5 traits of healthy masculinity you want to further develop. The traits should reflect a healthy model of masculinity. Your answers to the questions you completed in the most recent Customizing the Habit section might point to traits to consider.
2. Rate yourself on each trait. How much do you possess it? Use a 0–5 scale with 0 = "not at all" and 5 = "completely." Be honest and transparent.
3. Only if necessary: Identify how you can further develop traits you rated from 0 to 3. Get the input of others, such as your co-parent, a friend, or your accountability partner.
4. Only if necessary: Take the next steps to further develop those traits so that you can model them for your children!

AI Prompts

Here are two hypothetical prompts I created for holistic fathering and modeling healthy masculinity. These are only examples of how AI can be helpful in identifying ways to apply both habits.

- **Holistic fathering.** A skill I want to develop for my role in my family is learning how to landscape our yard. Acting as a landscape architect, recommend two or three inexpensive things I can do to start landscaping our yard that can start building this skill. I live in an environment that doesn't get much rain. We live in a 2,500 square foot house on a quarter acre.

- **Modeling masculinity.** I want to form a small group of fathers—maybe three or four in addition to me—to explore how we can better model healthy masculinity for our children. I'm concerned about how to approach fathers, so they won't be offended and want to join the group. Provide a sequence of steps for me to identify a good approach.

For the landscaping challenge, the AI tool that I used recommended starting with native or other plants, creating beds and covering them with mulch, and laying gravel or stone pathways. All three features are suitable for dry environments. To form the group of fathers, the AI tool suggested a 10-step approach, which included being clear about the group's purpose and goals, planning for potential concerns fathers might have, and starting with a simple, informal meeting format. It also provided five tips for approaching fathers to reduce the risk of offending them, such as focusing on shared values like being a good role model for children and avoiding a long-term commitment.

Chapter 5

Parenting Skills: Nurturing & Disciplining Your Children

"Children have never been very good at listening to their elders, but they have never failed to imitate them."
—James Baldwin, writer and civil rights activist

My mother was the disciplinarian in our house. She had to be, given my father's lack of involvement. She had no problem with using corporal punishment when I or my brother got out of line. She initially used her hand to spank us. As we grew older, she turned to firmer tools, namely a belt, the back of a wooden brush, and, my favorite, the sharp edge of a triangular wooden ruler. I hated that she spanked us. It was pointless. It didn't change my behavior. When I got old enough, I laughed it off, and she eventually stopped spanking me. I swore that if I ever had children, I'd never spank them.

I stayed true to my oath when I became a father, until I lost my temper and spanked Jillian. As you learned in the last chapter, Jillian was a terror as a toddler; she was defiant. She misbehaved one day when she was three or four years old. I don't recall what she did—only that it happened in her bedroom. What matters isn't what she did, but what I did. I lost my temper, sat on her bed, grabbed her by her armpits, placed her across my knees, and whacked her backside with my open palm. She was stunned before crying and running out of the room. After she ran out, I sat silently, shocked by my behavior, and cried. I couldn't believe I had spanked her.

After gathering myself, I repaired the damage I had done to Jillian—an important nurturing skill I learned from my mother. I told Jillian that I still loved her—and would continue to love her no matter what she did in the future—and that she wasn't a bad person for what she had done that led me to spank her. I also apologized for disciplining her inappropriately and in a way that was physically painful. I swore to myself and my wife, Kayla, that I wouldn't spank either of our children again. I maintained that oath.

Kayla was my co-disciplinarian. We acted as a team, knowing that children like to divide and conquer. Children realize early on that if their parents aren't united, they can manipulate their way into getting what they want. They often approach one parent when they don't get what they want from the other parent. They become sneakier about this behavior as they grow older. Kayla and I knew that, whenever possible, it was essential to communicate with each other about addressing our daughters' misbehavior before disciplining them. However, that wasn't always possible.

Our family vacationed at the Texas coast, specifically Port Aransas and Corpus Christi. We visited at least once a year, starting when Kayla was pregnant with Jillian. While Kayla and the girls loved the beach, I merely tolerated it. I didn't like how sand gets everywhere and sticks to you. What I enjoyed was playing with the girls when they were pre-teens and spending quality family time. When they became teenagers, I stopped going on every beach trip. This stepping away from this family time together—a nurturing act—allowed Kayla to further deepen her relationship with both of our daughters.

One beach trip when the girls were in high school, they snuck out for a bonfire organized by some boys they knew. When Kayla found out, she was furious. Because I wasn't there, she had to discipline them on her own. She told them that, upon returning home, they were grounded for several weeks. They asked her not to tell me what happened, at least not until they came home. I was fine with the grounding and not learning about my daughters' misbehavior right away. Effectively disciplining your children can sometimes mean knowing when to let the other parent take the lead. In that instance, she didn't need to involve me. I trusted her to respond to their misbehavior appropriately.

The two habits discussed in this chapter, nurturing your children and disciplining your children in healthy ways, will help build your parenting skills. The discussion will help you learn when the nurturing process begins and what thwarts some fathers' ability to nurture their children effectively, such as a lack of child development knowledge. You'll learn about self-worth's role in nurturing your children, the most effective style of discipline, and tactics of effective discipline.

Trait: Parenting Skills

The 24:7 Dad uses his parenting skills to create a safe, trusting, and nurturing environment that facilitates his children's growth and development physically, emotionally, intellectually, socially, and spiritually. He understands that increasing his knowledge of healthy child development will help him create this environment. He also understands that disciplining his children effectively requires using non-violent tactics to guide and teach his children about proper behavior.

You learned in the last chapter that fathers and mothers tend to interact with their children in different ways that seem instinctive, such as in the ways they play with their children. It's as if fathers and mothers bring some unique skills to fathering and mothering that magically appear. But there are so many more skills you must learn to become a 24:7 Dad! These skills are required of any parent or caregiver raising children, and they don't magically appear. Anyone raising a child must learn these skills.

One of the most worn-out phrases in books and other resources on parenting is, "Parenting doesn't come with a manual." That phrase is worn out because it's true, but only to an extent. Some people enter parenthood with a crucial experience that gives them a head start on creating their own manual: their parents had good parenting skills, including those of effective child discipline.

Some people enter parenthood with another advantage that gives them a head start when it comes to parenting skills, and they tend to be women because of the emphasis cultures worldwide place on mothers' childcare and domestic roles. Girls are socialized for these roles through play activities that are associated with those roles, such as imaginary cooking and playing with doll houses. As girls get older, they're more likely than boys to have experiences that act as on-the-job training, such as caring for younger siblings and babysitting. As a result, girls are more likely than boys when they enter parenthood to have already learned and applied some of the skills of effective parenting.

Men tend to be at a disadvantage for the opposite reason. Boys aren't socialized for childcare and domestic roles. Those roles are devalued for boys to such an extent that parents become concerned if their son shows an interest, or even a mild curiosity, in childcare and homecare. As a result of this socialization, most men become fathers with little or no experience in applying effective parenting skills and have a steeper learning curve than mothers.

Habit: Nurturing Your Children

The 24:7 Dad is a nurturing parent because he cares for the growth and development of his children, including their self-worth. Contrary to popular belief, fathers can be just as nurturing as mothers; it can simply look different. You learned in Chapter 4 that fathering consists of skills you can develop and refine. Parenting also involves a set of skills. Fathers use both skill sets to nurture their children. *Your willingness and ability to develop and refine your fathering and parenting skills form the foundation for nurturing your children.*

You also learned in Chapter 4 that self-worth is the overall thoughts (self-concept) and feelings (self-esteem) you have about yourself. The 24:7 Dad understands that building his children's positive self-worth—a nurturing skill—is one of the most important contributions he'll make to their well-being and that of his family. Children's self-worth is influenced by whether or not they meet the goals their father has for them. They learn to anticipate those goals and his reactions when they meet or fail to meet them.

It's fine for fathers to have realistic goals for their children. Realistic goals can help children learn to value commitment and motivate them to do their best in any aspect of life. When they reach those goals, it helps build positive self-worth. Unfortunately, many fathers have unrealistic goals for their children. When their children fail to reach them, it harms their self-worth. Some fathers react poorly when their children fall short of unrealistic goals, such as getting angry or using shaming language. Those reactions only increase the harm to their children's self-worth.

To help you get in touch with the goals you have for your children, it's helpful to reflect on the goals your parents had for you and how you felt when you met or didn't meet them. Complete the following statements:

- A goal my parents had for me that I achieved was

  _____.

- When I met this goal, I felt

  _____.

- A goal my parents had for me that I didn't achieve was

  _____.

- When I didn't meet this goal, I felt

  _____.

Your responses may reflect that you were deeply affected by the goals your parents had for you. A goal both of my parents had for me, which I achieved, was excelling in school. I enjoyed school and gained a lot of satisfaction from doing well in it, which positively impacted my self-worth. While this pleased my father, he placed a premium on another goal: he desperately wanted me to follow in his footsteps and become a classical musician. That didn't happen and, once he accepted my desire to pursue anything but that goal, he disowned me, which negatively affected my self-worth.

When Nurturing Begins

I've spoken to audiences nationwide about the importance of involved fathers to children's well-being. I've often asked those audiences to shout out which parent comes to mind first when they hear the word "nurturing." It's hard to hear "the father" over the deafening chorus of "the mother."

The reason that so many people in those audiences have said "the mother" is the belief that women are programmed by nature to nurture, while men aren't. *That belief is wrong*. Nature also programs men to nurture. Nature facilitates father–child bonding by preparing fathers for their children's impending birth and continues helping them post-birth. During the prenatal and postnatal periods, men experience changes in hormone levels and their brains. They experience a decline in testosterone and an increase in oxytocin that continues after birth. The decrease in testosterone allows fathers to have increased empathy toward their children, and more oxytocin helps them start bonding. (These hormonal changes help explain why some men experience a "sympathetic pregnancy," in which they can feel nausea, changes in food preferences, and other symptoms that pregnant women experience.) Fathers' and mothers' hormone levels can change in concert after birth. Fathers' brains also experience overall structural changes, such as reduced cortical volume, and respond immediately to the actions of their babies, such as increased activation when they hear their children's cries or see their children's faces.[1]

While being programmed by nature to nurture children provides the biological foundation for nurturing, fathers must be able and willing to bond with their children. That bonding only happens when fathers are physically and emotionally present. Ideally, that presence starts during the prenatal and postnatal periods by supporting the mother. This is the time when fathers can begin developing the secure attachment with their children that lays the emotional foundation for nurturing—emotional safety and trust in a parent, referred to as security.

Children seek this security from both parents. Contrary to popular opinion, the father–child bond can be nearly as strong and just as stable as the mother–child bond. An analysis of 95 studies on parent–child attachment found that when children formed secure attachments to both parents, the security of the father–child attachment was only slightly lower than the mother–child attachment.[2] Interestingly, the father–child bond can grow stronger over time. Another study on parent–child attachment found that the security of attachment remained stable and increased in both mother–child and

---

[1] Brown, C., Trahan, M., Garnett-Deakin, A., Pond, E., Cho, S., & Gibson, S. (2024). *Father Facts 9*. National Fatherhood Initiative®.

[2] Pinquart, M. (2022). Attachment security to mothers and fathers: A meta-analysis on mean-level differences and correlations of behavioural measures. *Infant and Child Development, 31*(6), e2364.

father–child relationships. While the mother–child relationship was secure in a higher proportion of infants, the proportion of children securely attached to their fathers was greater by the time the children reached preschool age.[3]

Forming the emotional foundation for nurturing in fathers when children are infants is not only important for creating the father–child bond, but also for maintaining that bond as children grow. When older children feel safe and secure in their relationships with their fathers, they're more open to their fathers' guidance. A teenager with a secure attachment to their father from infancy is likely to be more open to his nurturing than a teenager with an unsecure attachment to their father. But don't worry if your situation makes, or made, it difficult or impossible to bond with your children early in their lives. Using the knowledge and skills of the 24:7 Dad, you can bond with children of any age in ways that will help them feel safe and secure with you.

Regardless of when you bond with your children, you can increase the odds of forming the secure bond that's foundational for nurturing by avoiding two common pain points that can cause fathers to stumble along the way: a lack of child development knowledge and living vicariously through your children.

Lack of Child Development Knowledge

Reflecting on the statements you completed earlier in this chapter about the goals your parents had for you, what was a reason that

---

[3] Paquette, D., Dubois-Comtois, K., Cyr, C., Lemelin, J.P., Bacro, F., Couture, S., & Bigras, M. (2024). Early childhood attachment stability to mothers, fathers, and both parents as a network: Associations with parents' well-being, marital relationship, and child behavior problems. *Attachment & Human Development*, 26(1), 66–94.

may have kept you from achieving the goal you didn't meet? And how old were you at the time you didn't achieve the goal?

One common reason a child doesn't achieve a specific goal a parent had for them is a mismatch between the goal and the child's ability to achieve it at a specific age. The child wasn't ready developmentally. The parent expected their child to be capable of thinking or behaving in a way that wasn't possible for their child.

Your effectiveness as a parent is significantly influenced by your child development knowledge, especially of "developmental milestones." Developmental milestones are age-specific indicators of growth in children's physical, speech and problem-solving, and social-emotional skills. Knowing what most children can do at a specific age is crucial because it can shape your expectations for your children's capabilities. When you have realistic expectations, it can assist you in setting realistic goals and in managing your reactions not only to achieving those goals, but also to their behavior in general. This knowledge can also pinpoint ways to help your children achieve specific milestones.

For example, let's say you're a single father with an 18-month-old boy. You're tired of changing his diapers. You begin potty training him, but he shows no interest in using the potty. You lose your temper when he refuses to use the potty because you're convinced that he's ready to use it. After trying for another two months, you have nothing to show for your effort except more frustration and anger, and your son becomes even more defiant. Finally, you research potty training and learn that 18–24 months is the earliest that pediatricians recommend starting, and that the average age for children to become potty trained is around two or three years old. You also learn that the key is waiting until your child shows interest in potty training, rather than focusing on their age. You realize that if you had done the research before starting to potty train your son, you could have spared him from your potentially harmful and pointless reaction.

> ### Growing Fathers' Child Development Knowledge
>
> *Studies from different countries examining parents' knowledge of child development consistently show that fathers know significantly less than mothers.[4,5,6] To be fair to both fathers and mothers, there's a vast amount of information on child development, much of which is constantly being updated. We can't expect any parent to know everything about child development. But as you learned earlier in this chapter, men enter fatherhood at a disadvantage because boys aren't socialized to become fathers like girls are to become mothers. We expect them to know less about raising children. As a society, we must do better in helping fathers close this knowledge gap.*

To learn about child development generally and developmental milestones specifically, use credible, trustworthy sources, starting with your child's pediatrician. Most pediatricians today received child development training in medical school and keep up with changes in what we know about healthy child development, especially in physical development. A child psychologist can also be helpful, especially in social-emotional development.

---

[4] Baysal, Ş. G., Doğan, D. G., Kortay, S., Arslan, F. N., Öztürk, Y. D., & Yağın, F. H. (2023). Parenting knowledge of child development in Turkish mothers and fathers. *Trends in Pediatrics, 4*(2), 109–119.

[5] Aldayel, A. S., Aldayel, A. A., Almutairi, A. M., Alhussain, H. A., Alwehaibi, S. A., & Almutairi, T. A. (2020). Parental knowledge of children's developmental milestones in Riyadh, Saudi Arabia. *International Journal of Pediatrics, 2020*, 8889912.

[6] Scarzello, D., Arace, A., & Prino, L. E. (2016). Parental practices of Italian mothers and fathers during early infancy: The role of knowledge about parenting and child development. *Infant Behavior and Development, 44*, 133–143.

For general information on child development and developmental milestones, you can also use online sources with up-to-date information, including the American Academy of Pediatrics (aap.org), WebMD (webmd.com), the Mayo Clinic (mayoclinic.org), Centers for Disease Control and Prevention (cdc.gov), Zero to Three (zerotothree.org), Child Mind Institute (childmind.org), and Children's Hospital of Orange County (choc.org). Search for "developmental milestones" or "child development" on any of these organizations' websites.

As a result of acquiring this book, you can access another credible, trustworthy source of developmental milestone information. National Fatherhood Initiative® (NFI) has a comprehensive collection of developmental milestone charts for children from birth to age 18 that fathers participating in its programs receive. *You can download the charts from confidentfathers.com.* Enter the URL into a search engine or scan the QR code at the end of the Introduction. Developed and regularly reviewed by medical professionals, including pediatricians, these charts include a unique feature: actions you can take to enhance your children's healthy development. Fathers who have received this collection point to it as one of NFI's most empowering tools.

As you review these charts or any other information on child development, remember that your children will develop at their own pace. They may reach some milestones later or earlier than most children their age.

Living Vicariously Through Your Children

Before you read the previous section, you may have known early in your fathering journey that you lacked the child development knowledge necessary for nurturing your children effectively. You may have known this even before your first (or only) child was born or shortly thereafter. You may have also known early in your fathering journey about other factors affecting your nurturing ability, such as how well your parents nurtured you. But there are other experiences from your past that can influence your ability to nurture your children as they get older, experiences with impacts that can lay dormant for years.

Looking back at the statements you completed about the goals your parents had for you, were the goals you did and didn't achieve similar or identical to something your father or mother failed to accomplish in their childhood? If so, did they pressure you to achieve either goal, almost as if trying to correct a past regret?

If you answered "yes" to both questions, the parent with the same goal in their childhood was "living vicariously" through you. Living vicariously is a form of overparenting that can negatively impact a child. It typically appears when children start participating in organized academic, musical, and athletic activities and may continue through children's early adulthood. Living vicariously involves a parent treating their child's life as if it were the parent's own. For example, a father pressures or forces his child to play a sport the father loved as a child, even though his child doesn't enjoy it. (In my father's case, he forced me into music.) When his child is on the field, it feels as if he's playing the game through his child. When a parent lives vicariously through a child, it can hinder that child in becoming independent. It can also lead the child to experience stress and burnout from activities the child dislikes doing.[7]

---

[7](1) Reynolds, J. F. (2021). An intervention to address youth sport parent spectator behaviors in Louisiana: Lessons for future research and social work practice. *Child and Adolescent Social Work Journal, 38*(4), 463–474; (2) Brummelman, E., Tomaes, S., Slagt, M., Overbeek, G., de Castro, B. O., & Bushman, B. J. (2013). My child redeems my broken dreams: On parents transferring their unfulfilled ambitions onto their child. *PLOS ONE, 8*(6), e6530.

To see whether you might be at risk for living vicariously through your children, complete the following statements:

- Something I didn't do or achieve in my childhood that I regret is

  _____.

- The way I felt about this regret in my childhood was

  _____.

- The way I feel about this regret today is

  _____.

If you have a regret from your childhood and it's still affecting you negatively—such as a feeling of deep disappointment, sadness, or anger—you may be at risk of living vicariously through your children. To avoid living vicariously through them, it's crucial that you're aware of past regrets and let go of them.

Sometimes, it can be hard for a parent to realize they're living vicariously through their children because there isn't a clear connection between what they didn't achieve and what they're pushing their children to achieve. Instead, the parent has a general regret that influences multiple aspects of their children's lives. For example, a common type of regret is what author Daniel Pink calls a "boldness" regret. It's a regret resulting from a failure to do something that would have made your life better, such as more exciting or financially sound, because you weren't bold enough when you had the chance. Boldness regrets consume people because they ruminate on what might have been, which can drive them to try to rectify their failure through their children. They constantly push their children to take bold actions.[8]

---

[8] Pink, D. H. (2022). *The power of regret: How looking backward moves us forward*. Riverhead Books.

The signal that you might have a general regret that could drive you to live vicariously through your children is being so focused on what they achieve that you take charge or control of their actions, and you react negatively when they don't meet your expectations. For example, if the regret is your lack of boldness in going after what you wanted, you may push your children to be overachievers.

The good news is that you can use awareness of your regrets to avoid living vicariously through your children. Pink says that the true power of regret lies in using it to create positive change, including making better decisions. The 24:7 Dad doesn't allow his regrets to drive living vicariously through his children. He uses his regrets instead to avoid becoming so invested in his children's lives that he has difficulty separating his life from theirs.

Quick Win: Reading to Your Children

In Chapter 4, you learned that fathers have a unique way of reading to their children. Establishing a reading habit is one of the best ways to nurture children from birth. Fortunately, today's fathers read to their children more than previous generations did. But without knowing how to read to them, you and your children won't reap reading's many benefits. The most obvious benefit of fathers reading to their children is that it helps children learn to read. In the short term, it also helps children attach more securely to their fathers and increases their language and comprehension skills. Children with fathers who read to them have a larger vocabulary and can express themselves more effectively. In the long term, children with fathers who read to them develop more advanced social-emotional skills, achieve higher reading and math scores, and, for boys especially, better emotional regulation.[9]

---

[9]Cutler, L., & Palkovitz, R. (2023, April). *Reading with dad – influences on fathers' engagement in shared book reading and why it matters for children's development.* Child and Family Blog. https://childandfamilyblog.com/reading-with-dad/

Establishing a reading habit starts with creating a structure and environment conducive for helping you and your children focus on reading. First, schedule a regular time to read. Many parents choose to read with their children right before bedtime. That's fine as long as you and your children aren't too tired, and you can stick to the routine. Second, choose a comfortable environment that's free from distractions, such as television. Many parents choose to read with their children in the same location. Third, alternate reading days with your co-parent if your schedules allow. To give you and your co-parent a reading break, alternate or assign the days each of you reads to your children. Be flexible filling in for your co-parent when necessary.

After you create a reading-friendly structure and environment, here are some tips for reading to young children that maximize reading's benefits.

- **Read aloud.** Even though an infant can't respond verbally, they're taking in every word.
- **Read with gusto.** Be expressive and use voice inflection.
- **Make it fun and entertaining.** Use different voices for characters, such as a deep, booming voice for a serious or physically large character and a high-pitched squealy sounding voice for a nervous or physically small character.
- **Go off script.** Books for infants and toddlers are short and use simple language. Adding to the story with whatever pops into your head is a great tactic for introducing more complex words and sentences. Don't worry if your children don't understand what you add. It will help them learn more complex language.
- **Let your children hold the book.** This can be frustrating when children can grab and put things in their mouth. Be patient knowing this behavior will interrupt your reading, and you might not finish the book before their attention goes elsewhere.

- **Let your children pick the book.** Give your children two or three options initially. It's not important what they pick, only that they pick it. They might pick the same book repeatedly. Go with it.

- **Point to things.** When the text mentions a character or object, point to it.

- **Ask your children to repeat words.** If your children are learning how to talk, ask them to repeat what you point to. If your children are learning how to read, stop periodically and challenge them to read a few words or sentences.

- **Ask your children questions.** After your children start talking, ask them questions about the book's content that stimulate their imagination and test their comprehension. If they can't answer a question, or answer it incorrectly, give them the answer. Repeat that question the next time you read the book.

As your children age and start reading independently, your role will shift to encouraging them to love reading. Set an example by reading yourself (and ensuring your children see you reading), giving books as gifts, going to the library together, and reading the same book and discussing it. Consider creating your own "mini book club" by reading the same book as your children and scheduling time to discuss chapters.

Quick Win: Using Digital Technology for Healthy Child Development

A significant, growing challenge for today's parents is managing children's screen time. Nearly one-half of parents say they could do a better job managing (reducing) the amount of time their children spend using digital technology: television, computer (desktop or laptop), tablet, mobile phone, or any other device with a screen.[10]

If you're concerned about your children's screen time (or will be when they start using devices with screens), you're not alone. Nearly 7 in 10 parents cite it as their top concern for their children's health. These parents have a valid reason to be concerned. The American Academy of Child and Adolescent Psychiatry notes that children (age 8 to 18) spend, on average, seven and a half hours a day in front of screens and that too much screen time can negatively affect their physical and social-emotional development.[11]

As a result of this concern, many parents approach the use of digital technology only as a problem to manage and not an opportunity that can aid their children's healthy development, which is shortsighted. Digital technology provides opportunities for enhancing your children's development when you allow its use for appropriate motives, with reasonable boundaries, and in ways that promote your children's intellectual and social-emotional development. Specifically:

- **Examine your motives.** Make sure your motives for allowing your children to use digital technology are in your children's best interest and not to avoid fulfilling your parenting responsibilities, such as occupying your children's attention so that you don't have to interact with them.

---

[10] Woolford, S. J., Gebremariam, A., Schultz, S. L., Singer, D. C., & Clark, S. J. (2023, August 21). *Overuse of devices and social media top parent concerns, 43*(6). C.S. Mott Children's Hospital National Poll on Children's Health, University of Michigan.

[11] American Academy of Child and Adolescent Psychiatry. (2025, June). *Screen time and children* (Facts for Families No. 54).

- **Prioritize physical activity and face-to-face interactions.** Regardless of your children's age, don't let using digital technology replace the time for physical and social-emotional activities crucial to your children's healthy development. Children learn more from interacting with their parents, peers, and others in the real world than they learn from avatars in the digital world.

- **Match screen time to your children's age.** While there's still a lot we don't know about the ideal limit for screen time, the American Academy of Pediatrics' (aap.org) screen time guidelines offer a good place to start for establishing boundaries based on a child's age. (NFI includes these guidelines in the developmental milestone charts at confidentfathers.com.)

- **No screen time close to bedtime.** Don't allow watching a little television, playing a game on the laptop, or scrolling through social media become your children's bedtime routine.

- **Prioritize educational shows and apps.** While pure entertainment is fine in moderation, make sure your children watch shows and use apps that are educational and provide a rich learning environment. Common Sense Media (commonsense.org) provides recommendations on apps for children of all ages.

- **Use privacy and parental controls.** Parents worry the most about their children accessing inappropriate content. Most digital technology, channels (streaming services and others), and apps have settings that allow you to control the type of content your children can access.

- **Use digital technology together.** Whenever possible, watch shows and use apps with your children. This co-use not only means time together, but it also provides opportunities for discussion about what your child is watching and learning.

Two simple phrases to remember for the healthy use of digital technology are "less is more" and "model and monitor." Anything you can do to reduce your children's screen time is worth it. Model a healthy amount of screen time with your use of digital technology. That modeling includes limiting or completely putting away your devices when interacting with your children and other family members. Pay close attention to your children's screen time and the content they're accessing.

Customizing the Habit

It's time to customize how you'll nurture your children. This decision starts with reflecting on the following questions:

- How will I apply what I've learned so far in this chapter to nurture my children?
- To nurture my children more effectively, what parenting skill do I need to learn or improve the most?
- What else do I need to learn about child development? Where will I learn more about it?
- Am I so invested in my children's lives that I struggle to separate their lives from my own?
- Do I have a regret that could lead me to live vicariously through my children?

Customizing how you'll nurture your children can involve any one or more of the seven customization options in Chapter 1 that works for you. If you're already doing things that nurture your children, keep doing them. Remember to consider ways of thinking and actions you should stop doing that are keeping you from nurturing. And remember to consider habit stacking.

Habit: Disciplining Your Children in Healthy Ways

Disciplinarian is one of the historical family roles for fathers. A common portrayal of this role in television and movies is when a child misbehaves and their mother says, "Just wait until your father comes home!" But despite that traditional role, knowing how to discipline children effectively is a major pain point for many fathers. They can lack awareness of the skills they need to be effective disciplinarians. That lack of awareness can stem from confusion about what discipline and punishment mean.

Completing the following statements will help you start exploring this major pain point:

- The word "discipline" means
  _____.

- The word "punishment" means
  _____.

Did you have difficulty separating the two meanings? Do your meanings indicate that discipline and punishment are distinct but related in some way? If you couldn't separate the meanings or see how they're distinct but related, you're not alone. Many fathers who participate in NFI programs can't either. When these fathers learn the difference between discipline and punishment, they often cite it as one of the most helpful pieces of parenting knowledge they learn.

Teaching and Guiding Children

The word "discipline" comes from the Latin word "discipulus," which means "to teach" or "to guide." Many fathers believe that discipline means "to control." They think discipline and punishment are one and the same. They don't realize that punishment means to "penalize" someone for doing something wrong and that it should be a discipline tactic used in certain situations when teaching or guiding their children hasn't worked. They don't understand that punishment should only be a last resort rather than the first option.

So, how does a parent guide their children? By teaching them morals and values that reduce the need for being disciplined. Children become "disciples" of their parents. Disciples believe in and practice the morals and values a teacher (a parent) has taught them. Morals are standards or rules that guide what someone considers proper behavior. When parents pass down morals to their children, it guides their children toward doing what's right. Values represent what someone thinks is important or has worth. Parents use values to instill morals. For example, when a parent values admitting your mistakes and learning from them, it teaches their children that it's proper (moral) to apologize to others affected negatively by the children's mistakes.

When the 24:7 Dad disciplines his children, he recognizes that teaching and guiding occur in two ways: through what he says and what he does. He knows that his words and behavior must align. Many fathers overlook the significance of their behavior, how closely their children observe it, and the powerful messages it sends about what's proper and improper behavior.

Parents are their children's primary role models; the behavior they exhibit is observed and emulated by their children. Fathers in NFI programs learn the phrase "walk the talk" to remember that they're role models. When you walk the talk, your actions align with what you say to your children about proper behavior. When you walk the talk, you set an example of proper behavior that's crystal clear for your children. When you don't walk the talk, it can confuse them. Your children may wonder what's proper behavior. Is it what you say, or is it what you do?

Role modeling is an "always-on" parenting dynamic. You're a role model even when you don't intend to be due to your children watching your every move. It's helpful to think of role modeling as a "preventive" discipline tactic. The more often you walk the talk, the more likely your children will be to mirror your consistent, proper behavior, and the less you'll need to rely on reactive discipline or punishment tactics. Still, no matter how well you model proper behavior, your children will misbehave. That's when you must be direct and talk with your children about what's proper and improper behavior. That's where your *discipline style* comes in.

Your Discipline Style

Discipline style refers to the particular approach a parent has when disciplining their children. That style is heavily influenced by the way they were disciplined by their own parents. To help you identify your discipline style, let's start by completing the following statements that will help you reflect on how you were disciplined growing up:

- One time that sticks out in my mind when my father, mother, or main caretaker disciplined me was

  _____.

- What I learned from that discipline was

  _____.

Does your response to the first statement indicate that your father, mother, or main caretaker had a particular approach to the way they disciplined you, such as being heavy-handed and reliant on punishment or hands-off and reliant on your other parent to discipline you? How would you describe that style of discipline? If you had to give it a name, what would you call it?

Even though your discipline style is (or will be) influenced by how you were disciplined growing up, that doesn't necessarily mean you'll have the same style. You might have a different one because you didn't like the way you were disciplined. As I shared at the start of this chapter, when my mother resorted to punishing me with spanking, she used increasingly harsh ways to do that as I got older. I vowed not to do the same thing to my children. Depending on your situation growing up, your style can be influenced not only by your parents or main caretaker, but also by others you saw disciplining their children, such as an older sibling or relative.

There are five discipline styles for fathers:

- **The dictator.** This father is always strict, never nurturing. He's clear about his morals and values. He leads with control and enforces rules with an iron hand. His children know what he doesn't want them to do, but rarely what he wants them to do. This father says, "My way or the highway."
- **The king.** This father is strict and nurturing when needed. He's clear about his morals and values and leads by example. His children know what he wants and doesn't want them to do. This father says, "Let me show you the way."
- **The joker.** This father is never strict and rarely nurturing. He isn't clear about his morals and values. He jokes often and makes fun of his children. His children don't know what he wants or doesn't want them to do. This father says, "Let's just have fun."
- **The follower.** This father is strict sometimes and nurturing sometimes. He lets the other parent take the lead on discipline and backs them up when needed. He's clear about his morals and values only some of the time. His children know some of

the things he wants and doesn't want them to do. This father says, "Do whatever your Mom says."

- **The dreamer.** This father is never strict or nurturing. He lets the other parent lead on discipline and doesn't get involved with it. He's never clear about his morals and values. His children don't know what he wants or doesn't want them to do. This father says, "Whatever. Just leave me alone."

Reflect on your own discipline style (if you don't have children yet, imagine how you might choose to discipline them). Put a star or checkmark next to that style in this book. Once you've done that, ask yourself whether or not you want to keep or change that style and why. Write your reason next to your star or checkmark.

The king is the most effective discipline style. The king is one of the archetypes (unconscious thought patterns and behavior) of a mature man and father and is part of the overall parenting style called "authoritative." Research shows that fathers who balance being strict (firm) with nurturing and provide adequate amounts of both are more effective parents. That balanced style contrasts with "authoritarian," which is harsh and domineering parenting. Authoritarian parenting is ineffective and harms children.[12] The dictator is an authoritarian parent.

The negative impact on children of the harsh style indicative of the dictator is cross-cultural. For example, a study that examined the impact of parenting styles on 4,231 Brazilian children from birth to age 18 found that those whose parents had a harsh discipline style struggled to manage their emotions compared to those whose parents used less harsh styles. Children of harsh-style parents also had

---

[12] Sanvictores, T., & Mendez, M. D. (2022). *Types of parenting styles and effects on children.* StatPearls Publishing.

lower self-esteem, were less willing to help others, and had more relationship issues.[13] An analysis of 45 studies on parenting in China found that children of harsh-style parents were more likely to be defiant and aggressive, to shout, and to have attention-deficit hyperactivity disorder.[14]

The joker, follower, and dreamer styles reflect "permissive" and "uninvolved" parenting styles. While these styles might not harm children in the same way as the authoritarian style can, the absence of rules and the hands-off approach that characterizes them can lead to negative consequences for children, such as poor eating habits, obesity, and being demanding and impulsive. Children of parents with these styles may also struggle with emotional coping strategies and maintaining healthy relationships.[15]

The 24:7 Dad embraces the king style. This style might come naturally, or he might have to work hard to adopt it. Regardless, he understands this style's benefits for his children's well-being. He knows the difference between discipline and punishment and that punishment is a discipline tactic of last resort that links a negative consequence to an improper behavior. He knows the role of rewards, which serve as the counterpart to punishment, and how to connect a positive consequence to proper behavior, which teaches his children to value it. Most importantly, he knows not to use physical or emotional force in attempting to teach proper behavior.

---

[13] Santos, I. S., Murray, J., Maruyama, J. M., & Matijasevich, A. (2024). Harsh parenting trajectories from childhood through adolescence and socioemotional competences at age 18. *Journal of Affective Disorders, 351*, 61–69.

[14] Zhang, Y., Zhang, K., Yi, Y., & Shockley McCarthy, K. (2024). Does harsh parenting really harm? A systematic review of studies in China. *Child Abuse & Neglect, 149*, 106607.

[15] Sanvictores, T., & Mendez, M. D. (2022). *Types of parenting styles and effects on children*. StatPearls Publishing.

Avoid Using Force

Don't use physical force when disciplining your children, including spanking. It's simply unnecessary. There are other, more effective ways to address misbehavior that avoid the risks of spanking. You also need to consider the "why" behind spanking. In contrast to the many studies examining the effects of corporal punishment's impact on children, much less research looks into what drives parents to spank. However, there's enough evidence to suggest that several common motivators exist. Some parents spank because they were spanked themselves. Others spank because it's common in their culture. Still other parents spank due to their emotional state, such as being stressed.[16] If you spank your children or are considering it, talk with someone you trust. Discuss the reasons behind spanking before you spank your children again or for the first time.

> ### Spanking's Russian Roulette
>
> *If you believe spanking your children won't have a negative impact on their well-being, think again about the risks. While it's true that some children who are spanked don't suffer negative effects from it, many do. An analysis of 35 studies found that corporal punishment (spanking) increased children's violent behavior. Furthermore, the more parents used corporal punishment, the more violent their children became.[17] Another analysis of 45 studies found that corporal*

---

[16] Gershoff, E. T., & Grogan-Kaylor, A. (2016). American parents' attitudes and beliefs about corporal punishment: An integrative literature review. *Journal of Family Psychology, 30*(4), 453–469.

[17] Zhou, Y., Li, Y., Chen, X., & Li, J. (2024). Corporal punishment and the violent behavior spectrum: A meta-analysis. *Frontiers in Psychology, 15*, 1323784.

punishment led to aggression, depression, and anxiety in children.[18] *With other options at your disposal, why risk negative outcomes for your children?*

Embracing the king style also involves avoiding using emotionally harmful language in disciplining your children. Clearly, swearing at your children or calling them derogatory names is out of bounds. But there are other ways to use language that can cause long-term emotional harm. One of the most common of these ways is "blame and shame." Don't blame or shame your children by saying things like they're "no good" or "bad" for misbehaving. They know how they behaved, although they may not initially realize it was improper. They may also repeatedly deny their behavior and there may be others who share in the responsibility for the misbehavior.

When you blame and shame your children, they don't learn that their behavior was improper. Instead, they learn that there's something wrong with who they are as a person, a damage-inducing result. To avoid using blame and shame, it's helpful to remember the phrase, "Focus on the action, not the actor." Point out what your child did wrong, describe the action, and why it reflected misbehavior. If there were consequences that affected others or your child negatively, point out those consequences.

Use Reflective Reinforcement

Despite your best effort to discipline your children effectively without punishing them, it's unlikely that you'll never encounter a situation

---

[18] Gershoff, E. T., Lansford, J. E., Sexton, H. R., Davis-Kean, P., & Sameroff, A. J. (2012). Longitudinal links between spanking and children's externalizing behaviors in a national sample of White, Black, Hispanic, and Asian American families. *Child Development, 83*(3), 838–843.

that doesn't demand punishment. When the need for punishing your children arises, there are tactics that require children to reflect on their behavior, such as its effect on others, and reinforce proper behavior in the process. Some of these reflective reinforcement tactics can involve removing a child from the misbehavior as it's occurring or from the environment that has contributed to repeated misbehavior. These tactics include:

- **Saying you're disappointed.** Say you expect more of your child, and that you expect them to behave properly. Specify the proper behavior.
- **Paying it back.** Have your child apologize to the person they harmed, pay for or otherwise replace something they broke or lost, or do the behavior they were supposed to do in the first place.
- **Time-out.** Tell your child to sit in a safe spot, like the corner or on the couch, or go to their room for a brief period. Time-out works best for younger children between the ages of 3 and 10. A basic guideline is one minute for each year of their age. If you believe they've learned a lesson in a shorter time, don't make them sit in time-out longer than necessary. Use time-outs to help your children regain control, especially when they throw a tantrum. They should remain in time-out only until they regain control.
- **Grounding.** Don't let your child leave the house for a specific period of time. Grounding works best with older children, such as teenagers.
- **Removing a freedom.** Take away a freedom for a specific period of time.

Keep two things in mind when using reflective reinforcement tactics. First, avoid overusing them. Children can become so used to the same tactic that it no longer has the desired effect. Second, match the tactic to the gravity of the misbehavior. For example, if your child's misbehavior is minor, don't remove a freedom when simply telling them you expect more from them the next time will do the trick. Align the penalty's severity with the action's seriousness, as if you were a sports referee. In American football, a referee penalizes an offense 10 yards for holding, compared to 5 yards for illegal motion. In soccer, a referee issues a red card for a tackle intended to harm another player, compared to a yellow card for a tackle that could harm another player but isn't intentional. In basketball, a referee calls a standard foul and awards the other team free throws, compared to giving free throws and possession of the ball for an intentional foul.

To wrap up this part of the discipline discussion, I want to share an important behavior that every parent should use after punishing their children: repairing the hurt. Any form of punishment can emotionally hurt children. After you punish them, repair the hurt by assuring your children that you love them, regardless of their actions, and simply for who they are, even when they do something wrong and you have to punish them.

Use Positive Reinforcement

Fortunately, disciplining your children isn't only about correcting them for misbehavior. If it were, where would the joy be in raising them? Effectively disciplining them also involves proactively teaching proper behavior. Rewarding your children for proper behavior is a parenting skill that uses positive reinforcement to teach proper behavior. (Think of it as a preventive skill, like role modeling.) Before offering any reward, explain to your children exactly what they must do to earn it and the reward they'll receive. Above all, make sure to follow through. Don't promise a reward for proper behavior and then fail to provide it when your child exhibits the behavior. Some effective rewards include:

- **Praise.** Telling your child how much you like their proper behavior and that it reflects good character.
- **Touch.** Giving your child a hug, a massage, a gentle pat on the back, or a high five.
- **Freedoms.** Giving your child a new freedom they can enjoy either once or on a regular basis, such as staying up or out later, reading an extra story at bedtime, deciding which outfit to wear to worship service, or receiving money for completing an extra chore.
- **Presents.** Giving your child a toy, stickers, a new phone, or some extra cash.

It's hard to give your children too much praise and too many hugs but use freedoms and presents sparingly. Rewarding your children can bring you joy, which makes it tempting to reward them often. But rewards are a form of extrinsic motivation which, as you learned in Chapter 4, is a type of motivation that doesn't last. You want your children to develop intrinsic motivation to behave properly, rather than seeking external validation for that behavior. *Helping your children build a foundation for intrinsic motivation is one of the most powerful gifts you'll ever give them.*

Fathering's Long Game

Ideally, your children should come to value proper behavior without your guidance. That level of independence requires intrinsic motivation. A primary reason for helping your children develop intrinsic motivation is what I call "Fathering's Long Game." That long game is raising children who become adults with autonomy and purpose. Autonomy refers to a person's ability to act independently, guided by morals and values. Purpose refers to a calling or reason for existing or doing something. Author Daniel Pink explains that autonomy and purpose are vital for fueling intrinsic motivation. Autonomy fosters the deep engagement necessary for a full commitment to a purpose in life.[19] Your ability to effectively discipline your children will assist them in developing the morals and values that fuel the autonomy needed to discover and pursue their purpose in life and the desire to excel in executing that purpose (mastery). The father's contribution to developing his children's autonomy is especially critical as it may be even more crucial than the mother's in reducing the risk of his children developing mental health challenges, such as depression, that can hinder finding their purpose.[20]

Your children need your help if they're to reach that level of independence and find their purpose. As your children age and express their desire for independence, it's crucial that you expand your toolkit of discipline tactics to continue helping them develop intrinsic motivation for proper behavior. Applying these tactics requires that you see your children as independent human beings and that you focus on Fathering's Long Game. There are three tactics that are particularly helpful because you can apply them immediately when you see proper and improper behavior: focusing on their motivator, focusing on what they learned, and teaching positive self-talk.

Focusing on a child's motivator is about getting to the root cause of behavior. Young children can struggle with identifying what motivated them to behave properly and improperly other than, "I wanted to." Older children may know that motivators drive their behavior, but they may

---

[19] Pink, D. H. (2011). *Drive: The surprising truth about what motivates us.* Canongate Books.

[20] Dennis, S. H., Gettler, L. T., & Cummings, E. M. (2025). Paternal autonomy support and youth internalizing problems: Examining unique influences and interactive father–mother effects. *Parenting: Science and Practice, 25*(4), 473–507.

need help closing in on a specific or primary one. To help your children identify the motivator, ask why they behaved properly or improperly. (There might be more than one motivator.) Let them know that you understand why they behaved in that way. If they misbehaved, this doesn't mean you accept the motivator or the behavior, just that you understand why they misbehaved. Whether you're helping them explore proper or improper behavior, don't tell them what their motivator should be. If they struggle to identify their motivator, ask what matters most to them about behaving properly or refraining from misbehaving, such as a specific goal or outcome they had in mind. Once they identify their motivator, help them latch onto it by reminding them when you see the proper behavior again or don't see the improper behavior.

Focusing on what a child learned is about identifying lessons and consequences. When you see proper and improper behavior, ask, "What did you learn from your behavior?" and "How did your behavior affect you and other people?" If your children don't see some or all of the lessons or consequences, point them out one at a time by asking if they agree with each one. If there's more than a couple of lessons or consequences they missed, share the one or two that are the most important to avoid overwhelming them. This tactic honors your children and makes it more likely they'll listen to your wisdom. You might be surprised at how much your children say they learn from their behavior and know about its effects!

Teaching a child positive self-talk helps them build self-worth. Children can engage in negative self-talk after misbehaving or making a mistake, saying things like, "I'm no good," "I'm not smart," and "I'll never get it right." Negative self-talk can be influenced by what parents and friends say to children after witnessing the children's misbehavior or a mistake, such as "you're no good" or "you'll never be able to do that." What children see and hear in mass media and social media can also influence negative self-talk, such as when a girl sees an idealized image of female beauty that doesn't reflect what she looks like. Negative self-talk demotivates children. Encourage your children to use positive self-talk instead, such as "I'm smart," "I'm going to do well on this test," and "I can learn this new skill," even if they might not initially believe it. Positive self-talk stokes intrinsic motivation.

Quick Win: Using Positive Reminders to Build Self-Worth

You learned earlier in this chapter about the importance of building your children's self-worth. A simple, effective tactic for building their self-worth is using "positive reminders." Choose a trait that you want your children to value and develop. (It's best to focus on one trait at a time, and your children must be able to read.) Let's say that trait is respect for others. Write "Respectful" on a sticky note and place it somewhere they'll see it daily, such as on the refrigerator or the mirror in a shared bathroom they use. Each time your child behaves in a respectful manner, put a star or checkmark on the note. Tell them how much you appreciate the behavior and explain why it shows they respected someone else. Ask them how it felt to be respectful. Avoid giving them a reward for the behavior; your praise and the good feelings they likely received from it will be rewarding enough because of the positive impact on their self-worth! Once you're confident that they value that trait, move on to another one.

Customizing the Habit

It's time to customize how you'll develop a solid foundation for disciplining your children in healthy ways. This decision starts with reflecting on the following questions:

- How will I apply what I've learned in this chapter about disciplining my children in healthy ways?
- What do I need to learn the most about disciplining my children in healthy ways?

- Do I use punishment as a last resort or a first option?
- Am I comfortable not using physical force in disciplining my children?
- Am I comfortable not using emotional force in disciplining my children?
- How will I use reflective punishment as a last resort?
- Do I rely too much on rewarding my children?
- How will I build my children's intrinsic motivation?
- *Before* disciplining our children, do I talk with my co-parent and try to agree on who will discipline the children and how they'll be disciplined? If I don't, how will I make sure to talk with them first?

Customizing your ability to discipline your children in healthy ways can involve any one or more of the seven customization options in Chapter 1 that work for you. If you're using healthy discipline tactics, keep doing them. Remember to consider ways of thinking and actions you should stop doing that are keeping you from disciplining your children effectively, and to habit stack.

Deep-Dive Activity

The activity below will help you further understand self-worth by reflecting on your experiences with it.

Parenting Skills: Self-Worth Survey

This activity will raise your awareness about who has built your self-worth, how well you're building self-worth in others, and whether you could be doing a better job building self-worth in others.

Complete the survey below. Place a checkmark in the boxes for all the responses that apply to building positive self-worth. Self-worth is the thoughts (self-concept) and feelings (self-esteem) a person has about themselves.

1. When I was a boy, the people below built my self-worth:
   - ☐ Father (biological, step, or adoptive)
   - ☐ Mother (biological, step, or adoptive)
   - ☐ Relative (grandfather, grandmother, uncle, brother)
   - ☐ Another person (coach, faith leader, teacher, a friend's father)

2. The people in my life today who build my self-worth are:
   - ☐ Father (biological, step, or adoptive)
   - ☐ Mother (biological, step, or adoptive)
   - ☐ Co-parent
   - ☐ In-laws (father or mother)
   - ☐ Relative (grandfather, grandmother, uncle, brother)
   - ☐ Another person (coach, faith leader, teacher, a friend)
   - ☐ Boss
   - ☐ Other co-workers

3. I build my children's self-worth with:
   - ☐ Praise for who they are
   - ☐ Praise for what they do
   - ☐ Gentle touch
   - ☐ Finding and nurturing their talents and interests

4. I build my own self-worth with:
   - ☐ Self-praise for who I am
   - ☐ Self-praise for what I do
   - ☐ Gentle touch (such as getting a massage)
   - ☐ Finding and nurturing my talents and interests

5. I build my co-parent's self-worth with:

☐ Praise for who they are
☐ Praise for what they do
☐ Gentle touch
☐ Finding and nurturing their talents and interests
☐ Doesn't apply (I don't have a co-parent)

6. I build my boss's self-worth with:

☐ Praise for who they are
☐ Praise for what they do
☐ Doesn't apply (I don't have a boss or job right now)

7. I build my other co-workers' self-worth with:

☐ Praise for who they are
☐ Praise for what they do
☐ Doesn't apply (I don't have a job right now)

Review the results and ask whether you need to do a better job in building someone's self-worth. (That someone could be you!) If you identified someone, decide how to build their self-worth. Before taking the next steps in building that person's self-worth, get the input of others, such as your co-parent, a friend, or your accountability partner!

AI Prompts

Here are two hypothetical prompts I created for nurturing your children and disciplining them in healthy ways. These are only examples of how AI can be helpful in identifying ways to apply both habits.

- **Nurture.** Acting as a child development expert, provide a recommendation on how much screen time I should allow my eight-year-old son to have. He doesn't have a cell phone. He has a tablet for playing educational and competitive games. I might be allowing him to spend too much time on his tablet. Share the source(s) you used to make your recommendation.

- **Discipline.** I'm the father of a 14-year-old girl who sneaked out of the house after her curfew. This is the second time she's done this. I didn't punish her the first time. Instead, I calmly explained why she isn't allowed to stay out past her curfew. I told her that if she did that again, I'd punish her. I've chosen to ground her. Provide a sequence of steps for me to identify a good approach for explaining the punishment and the reasons for it.

For the screen-time concern, the AI I used provided guidelines from an excellent, credible source, the American Academy of Pediatrics (AAP). The AAP's 2024 recommendations, the most recent at the time of writing this book, don't include a specific time limit. Instead, they provide guidelines for helping parents set time limits.

For the punishment concern, the AI I used recommended steps I could take before and during the conversation with my daughter. The before-conversation steps included choosing the right timing and preparing key points. The during-conversation steps included starting by acknowledging the sneaking-out pattern, reminding my daughter about the reasons for the curfew, listening to her perspective, and more.

Chapter 6

Relationship Skills: Communicating Effectively & Co-Parenting Relationships

"When people talk, listen completely. Most people never listen."
—Ernest Hemingway, author

Communicating effectively with others is an ongoing challenge for most people. Nowhere is this challenge more evident than in parenting. Communicating with your co-parent and others involved in raising your children can easily lead to misunderstandings, shouting matches, or worse. The importance of effective communication for fathers, and how often they cite it as a pain point, is why National Fatherhood Initiative® (NFI) has many resources addressing it.

I faced this common pain point with my wife, Kayla. The arrival of a couple's first child transforms their relationship. New parents begin to concentrate on their infant, the new most important person in their lives. After our first child, Alexis, was born, my relationship with Kayla began to change in ways I couldn't have imagined and didn't realize until years later.

The first three years of our marriage were child-free. Like many newlyweds, we wanted to enjoy some time as a couple before adding to our family. Those early years were challenging financially but not emotionally. We did what we wanted when we wanted. We had some minor differences, such as which restaurant or jazz club to go to on our Friday date night, but were on the same page about everything else. Raising a child sparked discussions about parenting that exposed differences in our knowledge, attitudes, and beliefs that had remained dormant. Those differences created issues between us that likely wouldn't have arisen if we had decided against having children. Those issues brought to light other aspects of my father wound and temperament, which hindered effective communication, particularly with someone I lived with day in and day out and had committed to building a family with.

For example, I didn't like conflict and confrontation; I avoided them at all costs. My parents steered clear of confronting each other, at least in front of me, so I lacked a model for healthy confrontation in a relationship. I knew that the absence of physical and emotional abuse was healthy, but I mistakenly believed that avoiding confrontation, even calmly expressed differences of opinion, was also healthy. When Kayla and I disagreed on how to raise our children, we'd discuss it first. Sometimes, one of us would change our stance because we recognized we were clearly wrong. Other times, our differences ran so deep that they led to verbal confrontations, often punctuated by shouting matches. When that happened, I retreated and buried my uncomfortable thoughts and feelings. I typically gave in and told Kayla that we'd do things her way, yet I often resented her for it.

Imagine being a construction worker or mechanic without the tools you need for the role. Why would you consider either profession? Unfortunately, people often step into a parenting role overlooking the tools necessary for it until they're compelled to acquire the tools. Before I became a father, all I knew was that I wanted to be a good father and have a 'til-death-do-us-part marriage. I was clueless about the skills (the tools) I needed to achieve both goals. I lacked the proverbial map to navigate from point A to point B.

My communication struggles with Kayla continued through the first few years of parenting. The problem wasn't a lack of self-awareness or intrinsic motivation to change my approach to communicating with her. It was the force of inertia keeping me stuck. It was simply easier not to change than to engage in the hard work that change demands. What finally helped me break through the inertia was realizing that my thinking was holding me back, not only about communication but my overall approach to relationships and life. My "mental models" sucked!

Trait: Relationship Skills

The 24:7 Dad creates healthy relationships with his children, co-parent, other family members, friends, and community. He understands that developing his communication skills is essential for solving differences between himself and others. He understands that the relationship with his co-parent has a huge impact on shaping his children's lives, and that the quality of the relationship with his co-parent is affected by what he thinks a healthy relationship looks like and how the world works.

He also understands that communication issues start with him and no one else. Not literally speaking, but from understanding that he can only control his behavior and how he reacts to others' actions. He's willing to question whether he caused or contributed to the issue. Even when someone else causes it, he reflects on how he might have helped create the environment that led to and is sustaining the issue.

This chapter includes two habits that will help build this trait: communicating effectively and creating a loving co-parenting relationship. You'll learn how to address common pain points in applying these habits, including how to approach and resolve conflict, how to be a better listener, and how to empathize with your co-parent. You'll also learn about the roles different parenting styles and power and control play in the relationship with your co-parent. But first, I want to share some mental models that will make it easier to apply what you'll learn in this chapter.

Mental Models

A mental model is a representation or explanation of how something works. These models help us make better decisions by simplifying complexity. They enable us to understand how the world operates. There are an infinite number of mental models that people use in decision-making. Some lead to improved outcomes that are more likely to be beneficial, while others result in poorer decision-making that raises the risk of harmful outcomes.

The following mental models will provide a foundation for completing the reflective activities in this chapter and identifying the most effective ways for you to customize communicating effectively and creating a loving co-parenting relationship:

- **What you can control.** When you interact with others, focus on controlling your own actions and reactions to how others behave. You can't control what others say and do.

- **What matters the most to you.** Focus on what matters the most to you when you interact with others, such as an overall belief, value, or behavior that reflects the kind of person you strive to be. (The deep-dive activity on core values at the end of Chapter 2 may have identified what matters the most to you.)

- **Let go of your expectations.** Release any expectations you have for how someone may or should react when you interact with them, especially when those expectations are unrealistic.

I've found these models very helpful in all my relationships. They've helped me avoid negative reactions during and after my interactions with others that can harm relationships, such as disappointment, frustration, and anger. These models helped me reframe the way I thought about communication and my relationship with Kayla. For example, letting go of my expectations for Kayla's behavior helped me let go of the resentments arising from our differences in parenting that had become entrenched and toxic in our relationship.

There's a fourth mental model that will help you in identifying and applying this chapter's habits: second-order consequences. This model explains that there's not only an immediate consequence of a decision (a first-order consequence), but also a possible consequence of that consequence (a second-order consequence), and a possible consequence of that consequence (a third-order consequence). The chain can continue. Most people don't think beyond the first-order consequence. While that consequence might seem beneficial, the next one might not be. By considering multiple possible consequences, you can arrive at different, better decisions or confirm that the initial decision is likely the best one. I use this mental model to help me more thoroughly consider the impact of potential approaches to resolving differences with Kayla and others. Before I recommend a solution, I ask myself, "What's a likely consequence if we implement this solution?" and "What's a likely consequence of that consequence?" My answers help me identify the benefits of potential solutions that I don't think of initially and can use to advocate for my approach. This model also helps me identify potential negative outcomes that cause me not to offer a solution that I initially think is a good one.

Habit: Communicating Effectively

Learning how to communicate effectively impacts every relationship in a father's life. Applying skills in effective communication will help you create the intimate, trusting relationships that will enrich your life. Unfortunately, many fathers struggle with effective communication, especially with their co-parent. This struggle is one of the most significant barriers to being the father they want to be, and why I've placed much of the discussion of this habit within the context of the co-parenting relationship. Nevertheless, you can apply much of what you'll learn in this chapter to the relationships with your children and others.

In starting the discussion on communicating effectively, I want you to complete the following statements that require reflecting on how you communicate with others in general:

- My strongest area in communicating with others is
  _____.

- My weakest area in communicating with others is
  _____.

- To better communicate with others, I need to learn
  _____.

You're not alone if you said resolving conflict is your weakest area or if you need to get better at it. (Along with my desire to avoid conflict, my lack of tools for addressing it when conflicts arose contributed to the communication issues in confronting my wife.) Many fathers struggle with resolving conflict. I frequently survey NFI's organizational partners about their needs in serving fathers to identify resources that fulfill those needs. One survey inquired about the pain points where fathers required the most assistance. How to resolve conflict with their children's mother was at the top of that list. We created a brochure dedicated to this topic, which quickly became one of our most popular resources.

It's not surprising that fathers need help resolving conflict. Research on gender differences shows that, in general, men and women approach conflict resolution in their personal lives differently. A review of 28 studies on conflict resolution from 11 countries indicated that, within the home, men tend to have a competitive and less compromising approach, while women tend to have a more compromising one.[1] Other research shows that men tend to use more direct, solution-focused language and often change the subject when conflicts escalate. In contrast, women typically use more emotional, expressive, and collaboration-focused language. Men often aim to move quickly to a solution, whereas women often avoid suggesting solutions initially.[2] Men also tend to withdraw more quickly, while women want to continue the conversation.[3] These differences can easily lead to misunderstandings, ongoing conflict, frustration, and anger. The inability to resolve conflict is an often-cited reason for divorce.[4]

Your ability to resolve conflicts between you and your co-parent, especially those that are ongoing, is essential to your family's well-being. The effects of ongoing conflict can be devastating for the well-being of all family members. An analysis of 71 studies on conflict between co-parents found that it negatively affects children's cognition, behavior, and psychological reactions to conflict. For example, children with co-parents in ongoing conflict often have lower self-esteem and coping abilities. They're more likely to blame themselves for the conflict and can struggle with their own

---

[1]Dildar, S., & Amjad, N. (2017). Gender differences in conflict resolution styles (CRS) in different roles: A systematic review. *Pakistan Journal of Social and Clinical Psychology, 15*(2), 1–10.

[2]Sack, A., Frye, P., Simons, O., Kang, S., & Cuellar, J. (2024, November 30). *The language of love: Gendered communication patterns in conflict.* Languaged Life UCLA.

[3]Johnson, M. D., Cohan, C. L., Davila, J., Rohrbaugh, M. J., & Margolin, G. (2005). Desired change in couples: Gender differences and effects on communication. *Journal of Marriage and Family, 67*(4), 868–882.

[4]Hawkins, A. J., Willoughby, B. J., & Doherty, W. J. (2012). Reasons for divorce and openness to marital reconciliation. *Journal of Divorce & Remarriage, 53*(6), 453–463.

relationship problems.[5] Another analysis of 230 studies found that the more frequently children experience this conflict, the greater the risk that children will have negative outcomes.[6]

Conflict between co-parents also harms the parents' physical and mental well-being. An analysis of 126 studies found negative effects of poor marital quality on various health outcomes for parents, including cardiovascular health, anxiety, depression, and self-esteem. Other studies have found that this conflict increases parents' blood pressure, puts stress on the heart, and elevates the stress hormone cortisol. These immediate effects can lead to long-term health problems for parents, such as weight gain, chronic high blood pressure, and high blood sugar.[7,8]

Approaching Conflict

The negative effects of conflict between co-parents drive home the importance of learning how to resolve conflict when it arises. The ability to resolve conflict is a crucial skill for communicating

---

[5]Rhoades, K. A. (2008). Children's responses to interparental conflict: A meta-analysis of their associations with child adjustment. *Child Development, 79*(6), 1942–1956.

[6]van Eldik, W. M., de Haan, A. D., Parry, L. Q., Davies, P. T., Luijk, M. P. C. M., Arends, L. R., & Prinzie, P. (2020). The interparental relationship: Meta-analytic associations with children's maladjustment and responses to interparental conflict. *Psychological Bulletin, 146*(7), 553–594.

[7]Smith, T. W., Uchino, B. N., Berg, C. A., Florsheim, P., Pearce, G., Hawkins, M., Henry, N. J. M., Beveridge, R. M., Skinner, M. A., Ko, K. J., & Olsen-Cerny, C. (2009). Conflict and collaboration in middle-aged and older couples: II. Cardiovascular reactivity during marital interaction. *Psychology and Aging, 24*(2), 274–286.

[8]Shrout, M. R., Renna, M. E., Madison, A. A., Jaremka, L. M., Fagundes, C. P., Malarkey, W. B., & Kiecolt-Glaser, J. K. (2020). Cortisol slopes and conflict: A spouse's perceived stress matters. *Psychoneuroendocrinology, 121*, 104839.

effectively. To develop this skill, you must first understand how to approach conflict constructively (a helpful mental model). Although I present the four-part approach for understanding conflict that follows from the perspective of your relationship with your co-parent, it will benefit your other relationships as well.

- **Conflict is normal!** Every co-parenting relationship has some conflict, but how you resolve the conflict is what truly matters. The ability to resolve conflict increases the quality of co-parenting relationships and supports raising healthy children.
- **Conflict can help you grow.** People often view conflict negatively, especially when they're unwilling to resolve it. However, conflict can spur you to learn and grow as a person, father, husband, partner, and co-parent. Don't run from it. Ask about every conflict: (1) How can it help *me* grow? (2) How can it improve *my relationship* with my co-parent? and (3) If we resolve this conflict, how will it *benefit our children*?
- **Know what you want, not just for yourself, but for your co-parent and children as well.** Before attempting to resolve the conflict, ask these questions: (1) What do I want *for myself*? (2) What do I want *for others*—for my co-parent and our children? and (3) What do I want *for my relationship with my co-parent*?
- **Approach conflict with a win–win mindset.** Avoid a zero-sum mentality where you win and your co-parent loses. The more wins you both achieve, the better off all family members will be. Ask of every conflict: (1) Do I need to win here? and (2) Can I accept what my co-parent wants? Resolving conflict is easier when both parties gain something from it.

By adopting this approach, you'll start to see conflict as an opportunity to improve the relationship with your co-parent. You'll also have the foundation for resolving conflict effectively. And, as a bonus, your ability to resolve conflict with your co-parent may lead to more involved fathering and benefit your children. A study of nearly 4,000 couples found that the more frequently fathers used conflict resolution skills, such as compromise, the more involved they were with their children and the more warmth they exhibited when parenting. As a result, their children were less likely to experience the negative social-emotional impact that the children of less involved and warm fathers can experience.[9]

Resolving Conflict

Now that you're prepared to resolve conflict, you're ready to use the six steps below to tackle almost any conflict with confidence:

1. **Identify the conflict.** Write down the issue, focusing on one problem at a time. Ensure that you and your co-parent agree on the conflict.

2. **Decide who caused the conflict.** The person who caused it should own it. Remember that you and your co-parent own the conflict when each of you contributed to it. Be ready to own or co-own it. You won't move past this step if either of you fails to accept full or partial responsibility for the conflict.

3. **Discuss the necessity of resolving the conflict.** Consider not just why the conflict requires a solution, but also why it's vital for your children's well-being.

4. **List the steps or actions the person who owns the conflict has taken to resolve it.** Write them down if the person has made several attempts. If you co-own the conflict, list the steps or actions both of you have taken.

---

[9]Gong, Q., Kramer, K. Z., & Tu, K. M. (2023). Fathers' marital conflict and children's socioemotional skills: A moderated-mediation model of conflict resolution and parenting. *Journal of Family Psychology, 37*(7), 1048–1059.

5. **Brainstorm other realistic ways to resolve the conflict.** If there are multiple options, write them down and keep them for the next step. Identify and discuss the pros and cons for each option.

6. **Decide how to resolve the conflict.** It's okay if there are multiple options. Allow the person who owns the conflict to decide how to resolve it. If you and your co-parent co-own the conflict, agree about how best to resolve it.

No matter how well you approach a conflict and follow the six steps to revolve it, you and your co-parent may not see eye-to-eye on a solution. In that case, you'll need to meet somewhere in the middle to resolve the conflict. That's where finding a compromise comes into play.

Finding a Compromise

If you've tried to resolve a conflict with your co-parent and one or both of you dug in your heels, refusing to budge, you might have reached an impasse and know how frustrating that result can be. However, you can find your way around an impasse when both of you are willing to find a compromise. Being willing to find a compromise may require that one or both of you discard a mental model that some people have: "Compromise is a dirty word." If either of you are unwilling to compromise, impasses become permanent rather than temporary.

If both of you are willing to find a compromise, use the five-step skills below to find a compromise:

1. **Clarify the differences.** Clarify that you and your co-parent have different solutions for resolving the conflict.

2. **Restate the options.** Restate your best option for resolving the conflict and your understanding of their best option or ask for their best option before sharing yours.

3. **Confirm their solution.** Ask if you're right about your co-parent's solution. If you're not, ask for their solution again and stay open to it. Avoid walking away or disputing that solution. They have a right to believe it will work, even if you disagree.

4. **Propose a compromise or ask for one.** You or your co-parent offers a solution that has elements of their solution and yours. Continue the discussion until both of you agree on how to proceed.

5. **Walk away if necessary.** If you and your co-parent can't agree on a solution, calmly end the discussion. Identify a time when you'll continue the discussion.

If you're a father with a history of conflict with your co-parent, I know how difficult it can be to apply the skills you just learned, let alone even being willing to approach your co-parent and discuss anything with them in the first place. Many of the fathers in NFI programs have the same difficulty. What helps these fathers move past this difficulty is when they accept that they have a role in creating conflicts and the responsibility to make the first approach in trying to resolve them. That acceptance will help you as well in the relationship with your co-parent. It will also open your mind to a potential reason why you contribute to creating conflicts: failing to truly listen.

Active Listening

The 24:7 Dad knows that failing to listen to others can lead to conflicts. Reflecting on your responses to the statement earlier in this chapter about your weakest area of communication, you might have identified being a good listener as your weakest area.

Being an active listener is essential for effective communication. "Active listening" is a skill that involves more than just hearing what someone says. Active listening requires focusing on the meanings of their messages and how they're sending the messages: words, sounds, and body language. *You can't truly understand someone until you shut up and become an active listener.* Listening also requires acknowledging that you've received someone's message and responding in a way that shows you understand what they're communicating.

Fathers can struggle more than mothers with active listening because of men's tendency to be "action-focused" listeners. While men and women can equally understand what the other person is communicating, men are less effective at providing feedback. They tend to be more distracted while listening and use fewer verbal and non-verbal cues to indicate their understanding of what the other person is saying.[10] Consistent with the different approaches that men and women bring to resolving conflict, men focus on identifying problems and solutions. Women, on the other hand, are more "people-focused" listeners. They focus on making an emotional connection, gathering details, and ensuring that the other person knows they're understood.

The Listening Filter™

As with research on gender differences about any topic, individual men and women defy the norm. You might be an outstanding active listener. Regardless, plenty of help is available for becoming an active listener. Just enter "active listening steps" or "active listening techniques" into a search engine (or AI) to find resources for developing

---

[10]Roebuck, D. B., Bell, R. L., Raina, R., & Lee, C. E. (2015). The effects of home country, gender, and position on listening behaviors. *International Journal of Business Communication, 53*(2), 153–185.

this skill. But that search won't help you find the barrier to active listening that I'm about to share, a barrier that can catch even the most skilled active listeners off guard at times.

Imagine you want to make your child orange juice from scratch. You carefully squeeze several oranges to release their delicious juice. The juice looks wonderful, but you notice it still contains the pulp your child hates. You pour the freshly squeezed juice through a strainer to remove all the pulp and...voilà! A happy child.

In that case, you purposefully used a filter to remove something that hindered the outcome you and your child desired. It was a conscious choice after coming to terms with the fact that your child hates pulp. Unfortunately, when we listen to others, there's a filter many men are often unaware of because of their inclination toward action and problem-solving. It's called "The Listening Filter," and it has three parts: criticizing, giving advice, and talking about yourself. This filter prevents men from truly listening and understanding.

To illustrate how problematic this is, I want you to conduct an experiment. Choose something, aside from reading this book, that involves listening and understanding. Options include watching an instructional video, listening to song lyrics, or having someone in your home explain something, such as how an issue they're having at work started. After selecting your option, take a deep breath and hold it for as long as you can while engaging with that option. Once you breathe again and catch your breath, quickly jot down how holding your breath impacted your ability to listen and understand.

It's likely you could listen and understand fairly well at first but found it more difficult as time passed. You focused more and more on your breathing and less on what you were trying to hear until all you could perceive was the pounding in your chest and ears and the feeling that your head might explode. You filtered out more of what you were attempting to listen to and comprehend.

The Listening Filter operates in a similar way. It clouds the mind to the point of obscuring what people are trying to communicate to you. The more aspects of the filter you have, the more it clutters your mind. To assess your use of The Listening Filter in the relationship with your co-parent, reflect on the frequency with which you use each of the filter's parts using the statements below. The frequencies are always, almost always, sometimes, almost never, and never. Focus on when your co-parent attempts to share or explain something, especially during tense conversations. Be honest in responding. Don't be afraid to ask your co-parent how they'd respond to the statements on your behalf! Write the frequency next to each statement if you like.

- **Criticizing.** I directly attack or subtly undermine my co-parent's knowledge, attitudes, beliefs, or actions.
- **Giving advice.** I tell my co-parent what they should do even when they don't ask for my input.
- **Talking about yourself.** I turn (shift) the focus of the conversation to me and look for opportunities to share my story.

When you use any part of The Listening Filter, an internal monologue kicks in for processing your thoughts. You begin thinking about what you'll say long before you say it. That monologue prevents you from truly listening and understanding. (It also prevents you from responding in a supportive way when someone shares an important issue they're facing.) You may grow impatient, frustrated, and angry the longer the conversation goes on. Eventually, you may feel you can't stand to continue listening to your co-parent. You interrupt them and launch into your critical, advice-giving, or all-about-me response.

If you realize you need to remove one or more parts of The Listening Filter, work diligently to remove that part or parts. Document your removal effort as you reflect weekly on communicating effectively. (Ask your accountability partner to help you maintain your removal effort.) Keep reflecting on how you might use the filter in your other relationships, both personal and professional. Do others use the filter with you? You might be surprised by how pervasive it is.

Body Language

In our discussion of communicating effectively, we've focused on pain points for fathers that may have been more obvious to you, such as resolving conflict and listening more effectively. But there's another pain point in communicating effectively that many fathers aren't aware of because it, like The Listening Filter, flies under their radar screen. Reflecting on how you completed the statements earlier in this chapter about your strongest and weakest areas in communicating, I wonder if any of your responses touched on body movements or expressions, commonly known as "body language." If they did, give yourself a gold star!

The 24:7 Dad knows that person-to-person communication is a combination of words, voice tone, and body language (movement and expressions). He pays attention to all three forms in himself and others. Furthermore, he knows that body language comprises more than half of all communication and words comprise less than 10 percent![11]

Unfortunately, many fathers aren't aware of how they communicate with their bodies or how often they use body language. As a result, they're oblivious to the resulting problems that lack of awareness can create. One of the dynamics in communicating with Kayla

---

[11]Lowell, K. R. (2025). *How much of communication is nonverbal?* The University of Texas Permian Basin. https://online.utpb.edu/about-us/articles/communication/how-much-of-communication-is-nonverbal/

early in our marriage was how easily she used my body language to discern my feelings during intense conversations. She was, and still is, very good at it. Sometimes, I would become angry and deny what she picked up on, partly because I was unaware of how my body betrayed my feelings. I thought she was off base and, as a result, I didn't remain calm during those conversations.

When it comes to body language, the 24:7 Dad uses it to communicate respect for others. This includes avoiding two common postures that many men adopt when feeling emotionally threatened, such as when discussing a difference with their co-parent, that includes being criticized or judged. (A "posture" is a specific use of body language and its result.) These postures are the "fight or flight" and "defensive/closed" postures.

Fathers adopt the fight or flight posture to defend or attack. A common emotional threat can arise when someone points out something in you that they dislike or disagree with, or when they urge you to change something, like your appearance or behavior. Fight signs can include narrowing eyes (looking angry), clenched jaw, shallow and heavy breathing, tightening fists, fidgeting, moving closer to the other person to occupy that person's physical space, and acting in an aggressive or threatening manner. Flight signs can include dilated pupils, widening eyes (looking scared), becoming pale or flushed, fidgeting, and difficulty staying still. When a father adopts this posture, it can result in him fleeing physically or emotionally, blaming the other person for causing the conflict, becoming angry, and dismissing or attacking the other person's opinion or something else the person cares about.

Fathers adopt the defensive/closed posture to shut down or withdraw. It's a different response to an emotional threat. Picture yourself in a heated conversation with your co-parent. They're blaming you for the conflict, and you disagree. Imagine tightening your arms, folding them across your chest, and pursing your lips. That action is defensive and signals a closure of your body to that person. Signs that a father is in this posture can include crossing his arms or legs, looking down or away, shallow and light breathing, hunching his shoulders, and moving farther away from the other person. When a father adopts this posture, it can result in him withdrawing from the conversation, becoming stubborn, giving "the silent treatment," and denying or making excuses for his role in creating the conflict.

A third posture, "open for change," stands in stark contrast. The 24:7 Dad adopts this posture when he's open to talking, exploring and taking responsibility for his role in creating a conflict, and changing an opinion or behavior. It represents a different reaction to an emotional threat. The contrast with the other two postures lies in how his body language signals his willingness and readiness to talk. Once again, imagine yourself in a heated conversation with your co-parent. Rather than crossing your arms tightly across your chest, you stand with your back straight, hands relaxed at your sides, and smile. Signs that a father is in this posture can include sitting or standing in a relaxed manner with his hands in his lap or at his sides, making eye contact with the other person, a relaxed jaw, slow and deep breathing, nodding his head in agreement, and otherwise appearing engaged. When a father adopts this posture, it can result in him asking questions politely, attempting to understand the other person's viewpoint, and seeking clarity when he doesn't grasp what the other person is trying to communicate.

Before reading the next paragraph, consider whether you adopt the fight or flight or defensive/closed postures with anyone. If so, consider why you adopt either or both of them. Next, consider whether you adopt the open for change posture with anyone. If you do, consider the reason.

Fathers participating in NFI programs often disclose that they most frequently adopt the fight or flight or defensive/closed postures with family members, including their parents, co-parents, and children.

If they adopt the open for change posture, which many don't, they're more likely to use it with friends, co-workers, and strangers. For most fathers, it's easier to be open for change and growth with those outside the family. If you want to adopt the open for change posture more often with family or in general, practice the body language and reactions linked to it.

Ultimately, communicating effectively requires the courage to admit how your body language affects you, what it signals to others, and how it affects how others communicate with you. It also requires the possibility that you might need to change how you use your body to communicate.

> ### Reading Others' Body Language
>
> *We've discussed the importance of paying attention to your body language, but it's also important for you to pay attention to the body language of the people you're communicating with. Others' body language can signal how they're feeling during a conversation with you. For example, your co-parent may adopt the defensive/closed posture during a tense conversation, signaling that something about the conversation is emotionally threatening. Noticing others' body language can help you explore their feelings, which, when not surfaced and discussed, can hinder effective communication.*

Quick Win: The Five-Second Rule

You can apply much of what you've learned in this chapter to rack up quick wins. Recently, I learned about a very quick win in communicating effectively. It's a simple method to reduce tension when a discussion becomes too heated. It's called "The Five-Second Rule." When a discussion with your co-parent gets too heated, taking a five-second break—walking away, for example—is as effective as a longer break of 10 to 15 seconds.[12] You simply have to be willing to use a five-second break!

Customizing the Habit

It's time to customize how you'll communicate effectively. This decision starts with reflecting on the following questions:

- How will I use what I've learned so far in this chapter to communicate more effectively with my co-parent?
- Am I a good active listener? If not, how can I become one?
- Do I need to remove parts of The Listening Filter? If so, which parts, and how will I remove them?
- Do I need to adopt the open for change posture more often? If so, how will I do that?

Customizing how to communicate effectively can involve any one or more of the seven customization options in Chapter 1 that work for you. If you're already doing things to communicate effectively, keep doing them. Remember to consider habit stacking.

Habit: Creating a Loving Co-Parenting Relationship

As you learned earlier in this chapter, it can be a challenge for fathers who are no longer involved romantically with their co-parent to apply the skills of effective communication when that relationship has a history of conflict. These fathers struggle with having the desire

---

[12]Fischer, A. H., May, R.C., & Donaldson, D.I. (2024). Both partners' negative emotion drives aggression during couples' conflict. *Communications Psychology, 2,* 73.

to even interact with their co-parent, let alone believe they can work effectively with them in raising their children. Many of the fathers in NFI programs who have a history of conflict with their co-parent must overcome their hurt and anger and develop the intrinsic motivation required to work cooperatively with their co-parent for the sake of their children.

If you're not in a romantic relationship with your co-parent, you might wonder why I chose "loving" rather than "good," "great," or another adjective to describe the kind of relationship the 24:7 Dad has with his co-parent. Loving emphasizes the importance of this habit. It reflects unconditional love and goodwill for everyone. The Ancient Greeks called it "Agape," rather than the romantic, passionate, and sexual love they referred to as "Eros." Loving relationships are easy in good times. A significant part of creating a loving co-parenting relationship is knowing what causes the hard times and what to do when they arise. As we discuss this habit, you'll learn about three of the most common causes of strife between co-parents and how to address them: differences in parenting styles, a lack of empathy for your co-parent, and issues with power and control in that relationship.

To help you start to explore the relationship you have with your co-parent, complete the following statements:

- The main differences my co-parent and I have in raising our children together are

  _____.

- The ways these differences affect our children are

  _____.

- Having power in my life means

  _____.

- Having control in my life means _____.

- Empathy means _____.

As we move through the rest of this chapter, I'll ask you to reflect on your responses.

Parenting Styles

You learned in Chapter 5 that discipline styles are more broadly linked to parenting styles. For instance, dictators have an authoritarian parenting style, while dreamers have an uninvolved parenting style. Dictators attempt to control and closely monitor their children, whereas dreamers take a hands-off approach and prefer to be left alone. You also learned that children of authoritarian parents often face poor outcomes.

What I didn't mention in the discussion of discipline styles is that fathers and mothers often have different ones. Likewise, fathers and mothers can have different parenting styles. An analysis of studies from 15 countries found that fathers tend to have an authoritarian style while mothers tend to have an authoritative style.[13] This finding isn't surprising, given traditional gender roles in many countries, where the father is often the disciplinarian, which carries with it the expectation he'll use an authoritarian style. This expectation is why some fathers can struggle to adopt an authoritative style. The good news is the role that two factors you've already learned about play in

---

[13]Zeb, S., Parveen, S., & Mahmood, A. (2020). Nonverbal communication in everyday encounters: The role of gender and marital status. *Current Psychology, 41*(2), 1041–1051.

adopting an authoritative style: fathering confidence (Chapter 1) and secure father–child attachment (Chapter 5). The more fathering confidence you have and the more secure the attachment between you and your children, the more likely you'll be to adopt an authoritative style.[14,15] The 12 habits help build both factors!

When fathers and mothers have different parenting styles, it often leads to relationship problems, such as lower relationship satisfaction, increased conflict, and more frequent communication failures. This can result in a *high-conflict* co-parenting relationship characterized by a lack of cooperation in raising children.[16] Not surprisingly, children raised in that environment are at higher risk of poor outcomes.[17]

Differences in parenting styles often reflect varying beliefs, morals, and values around raising children. For instance, consider a father and his co-parent disagreeing on how to discipline their 14-year-old son for shoplifting a pair of headphones. The co-parent believes that returning the headphones, apologizing to the store manager, and calmly discussing why shoplifting is wrong are enough to teach their son a lesson and reinforce that stealing is wrong. The father agrees with returning the headphones and offering an apology, but he feels that doesn't go far enough because stealing violates

---

[14]Kim, M. J., Park, S. Y., Choi, J. H., Cho, H.-N., & Seo, J. W. (2025). Factors influencing the confidence of fathers in their paternal role during early childhood. *Journal of Men's Health, 21*(2), 84–91.

[15]Zarei, S., Vardanjani, H. M., & Ebrahimi, F. (2018). Psychological factors contributing to parenting styles: A systematic review. *F1000Research, 7*, 906.

[16]Stolnicu, S., Darwiche, J., & Hendrick, S. (2022). High conflict post-divorce co-parenting: Understanding the dynamic processes. *Frontiers in Psychology, 13*, 913447.

[17]Lange, A. M. C., Visser, M. M., Scholte, R. H. J., & Finkenauer, C. (2022). Parental conflicts and posttraumatic stress of children in high-conflict divorce families. *Journal of Child & Adolescent Trauma, 15*(3), 615–625.

his morals so deeply. He wants their son to publicly admit to the theft by posting an apology on social media (not wise because it will shame his child). He also wants to ground him for two weeks. The difference in how strongly the co-parents feel about stealing has resulted in differing views on how to discipline their son.

Focus on Solvable Differences

If you and your co-parent have different parenting styles, you may have butted heads repeatedly over how to raise your children. (Even if your parenting styles are the same, I bet you still have some differences.) It's likely that some of those differences appear "unsolvable" due to deeply ingrained beliefs, morals, and values about raising your children.

By using the "what I can control" mental model I referred to earlier in this chapter, you can focus on addressing the "solvable" differences as a means to enhance cooperation and reduce the risk that those differences will become ongoing conflicts with your co-parent. Begin by identifying the differences you think are solvable. Those are probably the ones causing the least amount of strife. Then, follow the guidance below to embark on the path to resolving them one at a time. Before you request a discussion to resolve the difference, it's important to accept that your co-parent's solution is as important to them as your position is to you, and that their position might offer the best way to solve the difference. That acceptance will help you reflect on both positions as possible solutions. To resolve the differences one at a time:

- **Be clear about your solution and what led to it.** Why is it important to you? Where does it come from? What caused it? Is the cause a belief, moral, or value?
- **Consider your co-parent's solution.** Have you asked them about it? Have they said where it comes from and why it's

important to them? Have they said what caused it? Is the cause a belief, moral, or value?

- **Decide whether to accept their solution and move away from yours.** After reflecting on both solutions, does their position offer a better way than yours of solving the difference? Can you live with their position, even if you don't completely agree with it?

If you accept their solution, approach your co-parent with what they'll undoubtedly see as good news!

If you won't move away from your solution, request a 15–30-minute exploratory discussion to see whether you and your co-parent can solve the difference. This may be a highly charged, emotionally draining discussion. Limiting the time lowers the risk that one or both of you will become frustrated and angry, which hinders finding a solution. If your co-parent is willing to discuss the difference, use the following ground rules that provide boundaries for difficult discussions:

- No expectation of solving the difference during this discussion.
- Stick to the topic/difference. That's all you're there to discuss.
- Don't verbally attack each other. Don't call each other names.
- Don't bring up the past if it has nothing to do with the difference.
- Keep calm and end the discussion if one of you becomes angry.
- Depending on how the discussion goes, be willing to agree on solving the difference by accepting one of your solutions or finding a compromise.

It might take one or more additional discussions to resolve the difference. Remain patient. Even if you can't resolve the difference completely, strive to reduce the gap between your positions during each discussion.

Empathy

A major factor in building a loving relationship with your co-parent is your ability to see things from your co-parent's perspective. This requires understanding how they think and feel about your differences. That skill is called empathy. A lack of empathy hinders resolving differences. If you can't have empathy for your co-parent, you won't be successful in creating a strong relationship. It's that simple... and hard.

Popular culture highlights that females are wired for empathy and males aren't. As a result, fathers can question their empathic ability. If you're questioning your ability to empathize with your co-parent (or generally), don't question it. Neurological studies support males' empathic ability. For example, a study involving more than 140 men and 140 women measured brain activity in response to seeing facial expressions that evoke a nearly immediate empathic neurological response in humans. It compared those scans to the participants' responses on a questionnaire widely used in previous studies to measure empathic ability, which consistently showed higher female empathic ability. While the questionnaire responses in this study also showed higher female empathic ability, the scans didn't. When responding to facial expressions, the brains of both men and women reacted with the same speed. In other words, the more objective measure contradicted the stereotype that women have a more natural ability to empathize with others.[18]

Many fathers participating in NFI programs struggle to have empathy for their co-parent. Some of these fathers no longer live

---

[18]Pang, C., Li, W., Zhou, Y., Gao, T., & Han, S. (2023). Are women more empathetic than men? Questionnaire and EEG estimations of sex/gender differences in empathic ability. *Social Cognitive and Affective Neuroscience, 18*(1), nsad008.

with their co-parent and children, whether due to the end of a marriage or cohabitation, or never having lived with them. One of their biggest complaints is a lack of respect from their co-parent because they think their co-parent doesn't respect them as a father or a man. In return, the fathers disrespect their co-parent, creating a tit-for-tat dynamic that hinders cooperation and fuels ongoing conflicts. This mutual disrespect can also occur when co-parents are married or cohabitating with each other.

One of the amazing transformations we observe at NFI is fathers' readiness to be empathetic and resolve differences with their co-parent. Our programs encourage them to reject mutual disrespect as an option and to try changing their co-parent's mind, while accepting that their co-parent may never respect them. Fathers begin with examining whether they said or did anything that might have led their co-parent to disrespect them. When they identify something, they're prompted to view the situation from their co-parent's perspective and consider how to earn their co-parent's respect. It's incredible to witness the lightbulb come on because no one has encouraged the fathers to reflect on how they contributed to the disrespect or how they can reduce or eliminate it. Through this process, they start to develop empathy for their co-parent.

Valuing Your Co-Parent's Contributions

This empathy-building process also involves recognizing and valuing the different contributions your co-parent makes to raising your children. Fathers often focus so much on what they think is wrong with their co-parent that they overlook their co-parent's positive traits and contributions. To further build empathy for their co-parent, fathers in NFI programs assess their co-parent based on how well their co-parent displays 15 positive child-rearing behaviors in the list below. It's another eye-opener for fathers. As you read the list, think about the degree to which each trait or behavior applies to your co-parent:

- Spends adequate time with the children
- Listens to the children
- Respects the children's views
- Enjoys playing with the children
- Enforces rules and boundaries with the children
- Disciplines the children effectively
- Comforts the children when they need it
- Is a good role model for the children
- Respects their co-parent when with the children
- Has the children's respect
- Praises the children when they behave properly
- Shows anger in healthy ways
- Provides the children with healthy touch
- Builds the children's self-worth

How easy or difficult was it for you to assess your co-parent on those behaviors? If it was difficult, you're not alone. Some fathers in NFI programs struggle to step away from negative feelings about their co-parent and be as objective as possible in assessing their co-parent.

Quick Win: Activating Your Empathy Muscle

If you find it difficult to empathize with your co-parent, you might need help activating your natural ability to empathize. Use this research-backed approach, consisting of two mental models followed by six actions, that will activate your empathy muscle[19]:

- **Believe it to achieve it.** Believe that you can develop empathy. Without a growth mindset, you'll struggle to find the intrinsic motivation to become more empathetic.
- **Understand the impact of your masculinity model.** If you learned that men aren't capable of empathy or that empathic behavior isn't manly, kick that part of your model to the curb.
- **Venture from your comfort zone.** Proactively put yourself in new situations and environments that challenge you. Observe what others are experiencing.
- **Read fiction.** Practice putting yourself into the characters' shoes. What are they thinking and feeling?
- **Feel the bond.** When we take care of others and their needs, it releases oxytocin, known as the bonding hormone. Volunteer at a shelter for people or animals, a food pantry, or a hospital. Imagine being in the shoes of those you're helping.
- **Focus on similarities, not differences.** While reflecting on others' perspectives, identify what connects you instead of what divides you.
- **Ask people about themselves.** Asking questions about others' thoughts, beliefs, values, and meaningful experiences gives you a glimpse into their world. The resulting discussion fosters connection and understanding.
- **Question your assumptions and decisions.** Ask someone you trust whether you might be wrong about others and the decisions you've made based on those assumptions.

---

[19]Abramson, A. (2021, November). Cultivating empathy. *Monitor on Psychology, 52*(8).

After you activate your empathy muscle, it can take time to strengthen your ability to consistently empathize with your co-parent. As with using regular exercise to care for your physical and mental health (Chapter 3), keep using your empathy muscle regularly to create a loving co-parent relationship. In time, you'll develop the strong empathy muscle that's helpful in addressing another pain point that can stand in the way of a loving co-parenting relationship: power and control.

Power and Control

The power and control dynamic in your co-parenting interactions affects your ability to create a loving co-parenting relationship. Co-parents who don't share power and control lack a crucial piece of the foundation for this kind of relationship. They often lack a strong empathy muscle.

Reflecting on the responses to the statements you completed at the start of our discussion on a loving co-parenting relationship, what role do power and control play in your life? What does it mean to have power and control? Strictly speaking, power is the ability to exert strength or force on something or someone. Control is the ability to direct, restrain, or influence your own and others' feelings, emotions, and life. Power and control often go hand in hand.

When one co-parent uses their power to control the other, it can involve emotional or physical abuse. This behavior strips away the power and control that the other co-parent should have over their own life. Abuse knows no gender; both men and women can be abusers or victims. Although most physical abuse is committed by men, women can be equally or even more emotionally abusive. Emotional abuse can be subtle and harder to detect.

Here are 12 signs that one co-parent is trying to control the other using emotional tactics.[20,21] They may:

1. Isolate the other co-parent from friends and family
2. Constantly criticize the other co-parent, even for minor things
3. Threaten the other co-parent
4. Use guilt to control the other co-parent
5. Snoop or spy on the other co-parent
6. Be overly jealous or paranoid about the other co-parent's feelings and actions
7. React negatively when the other co-parent spends time alone
8. Make the other co-parent earn their trust
9. Make the other co-parent feel unworthy of love and affection
10. Constantly tease the other co-parent
11. Pressure the other co-parent into things they don't want to do
12. Try to control most or all of the other co-parent's activities

You have power and control over your choices. The 24:7 Dad chooses to help his co-parent, children, and others maintain power and control over their choices. He doesn't steal their power and

---

[20]Hogan, L., & Ratini, M. (2021). *Warning signs that your partner is too controlling*. WebMD. https://www.webmd.com/sex-relationships/features/warning-signs-sexual-abuse-teens-young-adults

[21]Bonior, A. (2015). *20 signs of a controlling partner*. Psychology Today. https://www.psychologytoday.com/us/blog/friendship-20/201506/20-signs-of-a-controlling-partner

control, and he doesn't allow others to steal his power and control. Applying the guidance from this chapter, particularly on active listening and empathy, will help you make that choice.

Quick Win: Signs of a Loving Co-Parenting Relationship

You just learned how to spot when one co-parent is trying to control the other emotionally, which is not a sign of a loving co-parenting relationship. Here are the signs of a loving one, based on the research of couples' counselors Drs. John and Julie Gottman:

- **A positive perspective.** Co-parents have a positive approach to problem-solving and can repair negative interactions.
- **Mutual respect.** Co-parents acknowledge each other's ideas and feelings and are influenced by them.
- **Openness.** Co-parents talk honestly about their hopes, values, and expectations.
- **Kindness.** Co-parents value and express gratitude to one another for actions they appreciate.
- **Repair conflict.** Co-parents have methods to mend their relationship when they make mistakes or argue.
- **Turn toward.** Co-parents respond positively when one of them tries to connect with the other.
- **Trust.** Co-parents believe that the other co-parent has their best interests at heart.
- **Commitment.** Co-parents believe their relationship is a lifelong journey.

As you can see, these traits can help co-parents create a loving relationship whether or not they're romantically involved. Even the belief that the relationship is a lifelong journey applies because they're raising children together.

Quick Win: The I Statement

Most of the guidance in this chapter focuses on how you can better understand your co-parent. You might be wondering how to help your co-parent to better understand you, especially when they say or do something hurtful. That's where the "I statement" comes in. I've used it with my wife, and she's used it with me. I statements are more effective when practiced by both co-parents.

An I statement takes this form:

- I feel _____ (optional) when _____ because _____. What I need is _____.

The wonder of an I statement is how it can diffuse tension even in the most difficult conversations. One reason is that its structure helps you to own your thoughts and feelings, state them calmly, and express what you need from another person or a situation. This structure helps you avoid verbally attacking the other person and immediately raising their defenses. Furthermore, it opens the door for them to empathize with your position.

For example, let's say you and your co-parent agreed not to allow your 10-year-old daughter to have her first mobile phone until she turns 12. About six months into the agreement, you come home from a business trip and discover that your co-parent has bought her one. Your daughter is over the moon about it, but you're furious. A shouting match ensues with your co-parent. You accuse them of violating the agreement, and they accuse you of not asking them why they broke it or understanding how difficult it is to parent when you're away.

Instead of getting furious and verbally attacking your co-parent, you could use this I statement:

I feel *betrayed* because *you didn't honor our agreement about when to get our daughter a mobile phone.* What I need is *for you to come to me first about breaking an agreement before you break it.*

(Notice that this statement doesn't include the "when" portion. Sometimes, you won't need that portion.) After finishing your I statement, you switch to active listening mode. Since the I statement opened the door to empathy for your position, your co-parent may say that they understand how buying your daughter the mobile phone affected you and will talk with you first before breaking an agreement. They may calmly explain their growing concern about not being able to reach your daughter and vice versa when she's away at a friend's house, which helps you empathize with their position as well.

If you want to teach your whole family to use the I statement as a habit for difficult conversations, here's a habit-stacking approach. Choose a weekend to teach it to family members. Afterward, set a reminder to practice it alongside the habit of family members saying something they're grateful for at the end of each meal. Twice a week, before sharing what they're grateful for, any family member can discuss how they recently used an I statement. Even if a family member hasn't used one recently, they're reminded of its value when other members share their uses.

Customizing the Habit

It's time to customize how you'll create a loving co-parenting relationship. This decision starts with reflecting on the following questions:

- How will I apply what I learned in this chapter to create a loving co-parenting relationship?
- What are the two or three most solvable problems with my co-parent?

- How well do I empathize with my co-parent and others? If I need to improve, how will I do that?
- Do I have a different parenting style from my co-parent? If so, what problems does that create?
- How well do I help my co-parent maintain power and control over their choices? If I need to do better, how will I do that?

Customizing how to create a loving co-parenting relationship can involve any one or more of the seven options in Chapter 1 that work for you. If you're already doing things that create a loving co-parenting relationship, keep doing them. Remember to consider habit stacking.

As we start wrapping up our discussion about communicating effectively and creating a loving co-parenting relationship, I want to emphasize the importance of embracing two values that tie the two habits together: honest self-reflection and seeking to understand others. When you're honest with yourself, it's easier to be honest with others and for others to be honest with you. Being honest makes it easier for you and others to communicate feelings and opinions. When you seek to understand others, it will be easier to find solutions for the inevitable misunderstandings and disagreements that arise in the relationships that are most important to you. Embracing these values doesn't mean you'll understand or agree with what another person is communicating or solve every disagreement, but by embracing these values, you'll be more likely to see the blind spots—what you're not seeing in your communication and relationship with your co-parent and others—that can prevent you from being the best father you can be.

Deep-Dive Activity

In this chapter, you've learned about how developing skills like active listening and empathy can help you communicate more effectively and create a loving co-parenting relationship. Using those skills will make it easier to solve differences with your co-parent in raising your children and in other aspects of your co-parenting relationship. The activity below, designed with the aid of an AI that I used, provides guidance on another skill for solving differences: identifying the differences that you have the most realistic chance of solving.

Relationship Skills: Differences I Can Solve

This activity will help you identify up to three differences with your co-parent that you think are the most solvable.

Begin by writing down the main differences between you and your co-parent. Next, rank them in order of importance for you to solve. Then, starting with the most important difference, go down your list using the following criteria for identifying the most solvable differences. (Most of the criteria are based on the work of couples' counselors Drs. John and Julie Gottman.) The more criteria the difference meets, the more solvable it is.

- **Duty-focused, not person-focused.** The difference involves a specific duty (responsibility) rather than a difference in personality, values, or lifestyle. An example of a duty-focused difference is disagreeing about how to divide household chores, who should pick up a child from school, and where to vacation.

- **Surface level, not deep-rooted.** The difference doesn't reflect or isn't manufactured by a larger, ongoing struggle or unmet emotional need that may also produce other differences. If the difference reflects an ongoing resentment, for example, it will be difficult to solve without first dealing with the resentment.

- **Emotional waves, not emotional tsunamis.** Any difference can cause an emotional reaction, but solvable ones tend to cause mild reactions, such as frustration. Unsolvable ones lead to strong reactions, such as intense anger, complete denial of responsibility by you or your co-parent in causing the difference, verbal attacks, and complete emotional or physical withdrawal.

- **Calmness, compassion, and laughter.** You can more easily solve differences when you can discuss them calmly, have compassion for your co-parent's reason for their solution, and even find some humor in the situation.
- **No sequels.** The difference doesn't keep arising over and over again with no progress in solving it.
- **Compromise is realistic.** You can foresee a clear solution somewhere in between how you want to solve the difference and what you think is your co-parent's solution. If they've shared their solution and you can foresee a compromise, even better.

If your co-parent participates in this exercise with you, it may be easier to identify the solvable differences and how to solve them!

AI Prompts

Here are two hypothetical prompts that I created for communicating effectively and creating a loving co-parent relationship. These are only examples of how AI can be helpful in identifying ways to apply both habits.

- **Communication.** My partner and I take a trip every year without our children. When we talked about possible destinations this year, we couldn't decide on one. We agreed to take a week before talking again and seeing if we can reach an agreement. I feel very strongly about my preferred destination, but I could live with my partner's. I'm struggling with whether to express the strength of my feeling before we decide where to go or simply tell my partner we'll go where they want. Provide a sequence of steps to help me decide, before we talk again, whether or not to continue advocating for my destination, keeping in mind that I want to thoughtfully consider my partner's destination.

- **Co-parent relationship.** Acting as a couple's counselor, advise me on how to bring a more positive perspective to discussions with my co-parent that involve solving our differences, especially in how we raise our children. Please give me your top three tips based on what the psychological research shows will help me bring this perspective to future discussions.

For the communication struggle, the AI I used recommended that I answer three questions to help me decide whether to continue advocating for my position: What do each of us want to get out of the trip? Is my preferred destination the only place that can fulfill what I want out of the trip? Which destination is best for our happiness as a couple rather than only my happiness? The AI also provided a sample script for me to use if I decide to advocate for my destination or go with my partner's choice.

For the co-parent relationship discussion, the AI I used recommended three tips that draw from Dr. John Gottman's research on effective communication. The first tip is for me to appreciate everything my co-parent is doing in raising our children rather than focus on why I think that my co-parent's position is wrong. The second tip is for me to focus on what's best for the children rather than on which co-parent's position is the right one. The third tip is for me to set aside any strong feelings I have about the difference before having the next discussion. The AI also provided research backing up each tip and a technique for applying each tip, such as using a "soft start-up" statement for any conversation that I can use to show appreciation for my co-parent's efforts in raising our children.

Chapter 7

Stewardship: Paying It Forward and Engaging Your Community

"Service to others is the rent you pay for your room here on earth."

—Muhammad Ali, boxer

In more than 30 years of helping fathers in various situations, I've encountered hundreds of amazing men and women committed to ensuring that as many children as possible grow up with an involved father in their lives. Some of these people have supported fathers in roles for the organizations National Fatherhood Initiative® (NFI) partners with to make sure fathers have the programs and other assistance to be the best fathers they can be.

Some of the people committed to supporting fathers came from the ranks of the fathers who completed NFI programs. After program completion, these fathers wanted to learn even more about being involved fathers, stay connected with the other fathers (and staff) they met, and proactively share what they learned with other fathers who were struggling like they once did. These fathers also wanted to give back to the organizations that supported them and helped transform their lives and the lives of their families. In describing the desire of these fathers to stay connected, a staff member in a partner organization told me, "We couldn't get the guys to leave. We had graduates coming back to the next class cycle and would drop in." A staff member in another partner organization pointed to these fathers' desire to reciprocate, "Guys that really got transformed wanted to give back to the community, so we came together around that common purpose—not just their individual experiences, but the impact in the community of father absence."

NFI's partner organizations often say that a father "graduates" from the NFI fatherhood programs they use. As a result, these fathers became program "alumni" who wanted to give back by helping the organization that helped them in any way they could to support fathers served by the organization and their community at large. Some organizations responded by hiring alumni to lead the program they graduated from!

Other organizations responded to alumni's desire to give back by establishing formal alumni programs. Some organizations implemented other NFI programs so that alumni could deepen their learning. Others created volunteer opportunities for fathers to get out into their community and support other fathers, such as manning a booth at a county fair or human-services fair where they could connect fathers to resources that help in meeting basic needs, such as food, housing, and jobs.

When I learned about these alumni programs, I donned my anthropologist's hat. I interviewed staff who led the programs to identify the ideal approach for creating and sustaining an alumni program in any context. In doing so, I ran across many inspiring examples of fathers giving back and engaging their communities in many ways. For example, in an interview with staff from an organization in Minneapolis, MN, I discovered that alumni enrolled in a 12-week process to develop life skills, such as public speaking, and personal empowerment. These fathers shared their overall life experiences and growth as fathers by making presentations in various community settings, such as schools, childcare centers, government agencies, and to groups of business professionals, mothers, and youth. They also presented to staff in other organizations about the challenges fathers face and how to effectively engage with fathers. They also used the presentations to recruit fathers into their organization's program by spreading the word about how much it helped them and other fathers they knew.

I also interviewed staff from an organization in Newark, NJ, where alumni participated in orientation meetings for fathers starting the fathering program or occasionally stopped by program meetings to share their experiences regarding the program's topics. These fathers also engaged in community service, including painting a childcare center in partnership with Home Depot, which donated the paint and supplies. Alumni also hosted a barbecue at a different school each year for children with perfect attendance and who were on the honor roll. These fathers picked up garbage, weeded, and cleaned abandoned lots. On the first day of the school year, they walked children to school and handed out t-shirts to fathers of schoolchildren to raise awareness about the importance of fathers. They also helped another organization start a domestic violence prevention program.

These formal alumni programs created on ramps for applying the habits of stewardship—paying it forward and engaging your community—that you'll learn about in this chapter by training alumni to recruit fathers into our programs, deliver (facilitate) our programs, mentor fathers new to our programs, and serve as ambassadors in the community by presenting on the importance of involved fathers. I used the interviews to develop a guide that has helped many other organizations launch an alumni program, providing more fathers the opportunity to pay it forward and engage their community.

Trait: Stewardship

The 24:7 Dad understands that he's part of a community of fathers characterized by mutual support. He shares the lessons he's learned about confident fathering with his children and other fathers by leveraging opportunities that arise naturally. He understands that contributing to his community by participating in its civic life helps create a strong community that supports the well-being of other fathers, children, and families.

The habits in this chapter involve using what you've learned about being a 24:7 Dad to improve the lives of other fathers, mothers, children, and families. Paying it forward involves being intentional and proactive in sharing what you've learned, one father at a time. Engaging your community involves sharing what you've learned with many fathers at once and supporting your community in ways that may indirectly support families. As you'll learn shortly, applying these habits is straightforward, except for customizing them based on your situation.

Habit: Paying It Forward

The 24:7 Dad shares what he's learned about being the best father possible—with his children and with other fathers. Paying it forward means passing along kindness to others rather than repaying the person who helped you. In other words, you won't repay me for what you learn from this book or other fathering resources. (Except for the cost of acquiring this book!) Instead, you'll share what you've learned with other fathers who haven't yet discovered these habits and tools.

The most common way in which someone pays it forward is by sharing a lesson or something else they learned with someone else. This sharing takes place in all sorts of conversations—planned and unplanned, short and long, and with family, friends, and strangers. (Some of the most interesting lessons shared with me have come from strangers I've sat next to on an airplane!) To start reflecting on the role paying it forward has already played in your life, complete the following statements:

- The last time someone passed on something they learned to me was
  _____.

- The impact that lesson had on my life was
  _____.

- The last time I passed on something I learned to someone else was
  _____.

- The impact that lesson had on their life was
  _____.

It's likely your responses show that you've had experience with how helpful paying it forward can be. In thinking back to the lesson you learned and the lesson you gave, was the sharing of either lesson part of a relationship designed to foster lesson sharing?

In addition to the informal nature that characterizes most sharing of lessons, mentoring is a relationship designed for sharing knowledge, lessons, and overall wisdom. Some mentoring relationships are intentional and planned, while some are informal, such as those between family members or friends that form organically. To reflect on the role mentoring may have played in your life, complete the following statements:

- The most important family mentor in my life was or is
  _____.

- The most important lesson that mentor taught me was
  _____.

- The most important non-family mentor in my life was or is
  _____.

- The most important lesson that mentor taught me was
  _____.

Was either lesson directly or indirectly related to fathering? If so, did your mentor share other knowledge, lessons, or experience with you that influenced your fathering?

Growing up, I was fortunate to have a few men and fathers show me that I could take a different path than my father's. These mentors gave me a glimpse, however small, that I could be a different man and father. As an adult, I've been fortunate to have many incredible fathers and business leaders teach and advise me on my fathering and how to succeed in running an organization that's improved the well-being of fathers, mothers, children, families, and communities nationwide. These mentors' positive impact has been huge, and I can't thank them enough.

Start with Role Modeling

When I introduced the 12 habits in Chapter 1, I said that you should wait to apply paying it forward (and engaging with community) until you have consistently applied the first 10 habits. I still stand by that instruction but with the following caveat. You can and should pay it forward to your children as quickly as you can.

Start paying it forward to your children by role modeling a 24:7 Dad, even though he's likely to be "still under construction." When it comes to your children, it's never too early to pass on what you've learned so far in this book about being a 24:7 Dad. You learned in Chapter 5 about the powerful effect your role modeling has on your children. Don't wait to start using that influence for your children's benefit. As your children grow older and you become an even more confident father, you can be more intentional and proactive in spotting opportunities to discuss what you've learned with them. For example, when your children start talking about having their own children one day, you could share the overall and specific ways in which fathers contribute to their children's well-being that you learned in the Introduction. When they have a significant difference with someone they want to solve, you could share the guidance on resolving conflict that you learned in Chapter 6.

Share Lessons Reactively

You also don't have to wait until you've consistently applied the first 10 habits to start paying it forward to other fathers. Recommending this book is an easy way to pay it forward to one father at a time. Sharing lessons reactively means that you're prepared to share what you've learned about being a 24:7 Dad when a father signals that he wants to talk about fathering in general or wants guidance on addressing a fathering pain point. This signal will arise naturally in your interactions with other fathers. For example, if a father who works with you shares his struggle with work–family balance and asks for your advice on finding that balance, seize that opportunity to share the work–family balance guidance you learned in Chapter 3 and any successful tactics you've used.

When you pay it forward to other fathers reactively, you're not looking to form ongoing mentoring relationships. You're simply sharing lessons whenever opportunities arise. You can share lessons learned with a father of any age, at any time, and in any place, and with a father inside or outside your family. I hope you'll share lessons whenever unplanned opportunities arise!

Mentor Fathers in Your Circle of Influence

After you've applied the first 10 habits, are confident that you've applied them well, and have experienced their positive impact, you're ready to start paying it forward by proactively forming ongoing mentoring relationships with other fathers, starting with those in your "circle of influence."

Fathers in your circle of influence are those you have relationships with, or could develop relationships with, because you're connected to them through formal or informal ties. Your path and theirs may cross frequently or infrequently, and they may be friends or acquaintances. These fathers are in your personal and professional networks, such as relatives and co-workers. They attend your place of worship, live in your neighborhood, go to the gym where you work out, and have children that attend the same schools as your children.

When you're ready to pay it forward through an ongoing mentoring relationship, you can start a relationship reactively by waiting for a father to signal he wants guidance, such as the example of the father struggling with work–family balance in the previous section. But instead of sharing a lesson and moving on, you intentionally use that opportunity to discuss an ongoing mentoring relationship. You can also start forming a mentoring relationship by not waiting for a father you know may need guidance and proactively offering your guidance, such as your best friend who you know is struggling with disciplining his teenage son.

If you're an extrovert, offering your guidance reactively or proactively may come easily. (In fact, you may have already done so!) If you're an introvert, offering your guidance to another father, especially proactively, may require stepping out of your comfort zone, especially if the father is only an acquaintance. You may be most comfortable being reactive, at least until you provide a few fathers with guidance and see how valuable that guidance can be!

Proactive Mentoring

To proactively identify a father to mentor, start by asking yourself whether any of the fathers in your circle of influence have mentioned, even casually, that they have fathering challenges. Keep in mind that fathers may not discuss their struggles openly. You might need to act like a private investigator to determine if there's a way for you to assist a father. You can strike up a casual conversation with another father by sharing an experience with your children, such as going to an event together, and seeing how he responds. You can also share a struggle you're having, such as difficulty helping your child with a school subject, and asking if he has any advice for you.

After you identify a father, focus on opening the door for your guidance, unless he's opened the door already by asking you for help. But if he hasn't asked for your guidance, don't rush in like "Dad Perfect" spewing your wisdom. Building a solid mentoring relationship can take time. In fact, research shows that the most effective mentoring relationships are longer ones.[1,2] Your first and most vital job is to build trust with the father. You may have heard the mantra, "No one cares how much you know, until they know how much you care." That mantra applies here; don't rush to be the mentor a father never had. Resist the urge to offer guidance right off the bat. Show him you care about him as a person and his success in all aspects of his life. Tread lightly until the father indicates that he's ready for your

---

[1] Grossman, J. B., & Rhodes, J. E. (2002). The test of time: Predictors and effects of duration in youth mentoring relationships. *American Journal of Community Psychology, 30*(2), 199–219.

[2] Allen, T. D., & Eby, L. T. (2003). Relationship effectiveness for mentors: Factors associated with learning and quality. *Journal of Management, 29*(4), 469–486.

mentoring. You'll know he's ready for guidance when he approaches you with questions about his fathering challenges.

When the father is ready for your guidance, take baby steps. Allow the mentoring aspect of your relationship to evolve naturally. Let him know at first that you have some experience as a father and that you'd appreciate the chance to discuss what he's experiencing. Begin by sharing a struggle you faced and how you managed to overcome it, especially if a mentor of yours helped you overcome it. When approached in this gentle manner, he'll likely be open to your guidance. When he asks you for help with a specific challenge, provide your guidance and leave it at that until he asks for help again.

Check in with the father from time to time to see how helpful your guidance was. If it was helpful, ask if you can help him with any other fathering issues he may be facing, or if he'd like to get together and discuss his and your fathering experiences generally. Getting together and talking about your respective experiences can benefit both of you and help you form a stronger bond.

Mentoring's ROI

Mentoring can have a significant return on investment (ROI) for you. View mentoring other fathers as the next step in your growth. It will not only benefit any father you mentor; it will also enhance your well-being. Research on mentoring shows it can have huge ROI by further building mentors' self-worth, leading to greater satisfaction from positively impacting future generations, and providing new insights.[3] It can also

---

[3]Hill, S. E. M., Ward, W. L., Seay, A., & Buzenski, J. (2022). The nature and evolution of the mentoring relationship in academic health centers. *Journal of Clinical Psychology in Medical Settings, 29*(3), 557–569.

build mentors' leadership confidence.[4] When men mentor other men, it can encourage mentors to re-examine their masculine model, such as being more open and trusting in relationships.[5] To learn about effective mentoring relationships, here are some excellent online resources: National Mentoring Resource Center (nationalmentoringresourcecenter.org), *MENTOR* (mentoring.org), *and the American Psychological Association* (apa.org/education-career/grad/mentoring).

Quick Win: Mind the Age Gap

If there's a large age gap between you and a father you want to mentor, account for the differences in the ways that fathers across generations can see and experience the world generally and in fathering specifically. This dynamic applies whether the father is younger or older than you. Men are becoming fathers at older ages than ever before. Today, it's not uncommon for fathers in their 40s and 50s to have toddlers running around. They may benefit from being mentored by a younger father with more fathering experience!

You learned in the Introduction that the fathering role is rapidly evolving. Before offering advice to a much younger or older father, take the time to listen to his fathering experience and explore his world and that of his children. Once you grasp where he's coming from, you'll be better positioned to provide guidance that he'll embrace.

---

[4]Ayoobzadeh, M., & Boies, K. (2020). From mentors to leaders: Leader development outcomes for mentors. *Journal of Managerial Psychology, 35*(6), 497–511.

[5]Henderson, M., Hughes, M., Hurley, J., & Smith, G. (2022). Voluntary male mentors' lived experience of social engagement with men in their community. *Health & Social Care in the Community, 31*(2), e423–e430.

Customizing the Habit

It's time to customize how you'll pay it forward. This decision starts with reflecting on the following questions:

- How will I apply what I've learned so far in this chapter about paying it forward?
- Am I willing to provide guidance reactively?
- Am I willing to provide guidance proactively?
- If I'm willing to be proactive, which father in my circle of influence might be open to mentoring?
- If I decide to mentor a father in my circle of influence—and he indicates that he's ready for my guidance—how will I frame my guidance in a way that will encourage him to consider it?

Customizing paying it forward can involve any of the following customization options from Chapter 1 that work for you: me and my family, me and my friends, and me and my community. If you're already doing things that pay it forward, keep doing them. Remember to consider habit stacking.

Habit: Engaging Your Community

One of the amazing people I've encountered in my work with NFI is a father and city government official in Texas. He was concerned about the negative impact of drug use on the city's youth population, particularly the impact of the opioid epidemic and other drugs. In researching factors that contributed to drug use, he learned that youth who grow up without involved fathers in their lives are much more likely to use drugs.

This father decided to launch a city-wide initiative to reduce drug use by increasing fathers' involvement, but he needed funding and an approach for mobilizing the city's leaders and other residents to buy into it and get involved. To fund the initiative, he used the link between the lack of involved fathers and youth drug use to acquire funding dedicated to combatting opioid use. In searching for an approach to mobilize his city, he learned about NFI's community mobilization approach (CMA) that other communities have used to establish father-involvement initiatives.

He used the CMA to accomplish three steps that were essential to mobilizing his city: identifying the assets (resources) the city could mobilize in starting the initiative, mobilizing sectors across the community to get involved, and selecting an organization to lead the initiative after implementation. The primary asset this father identified was a small group of community leaders that spearheaded the initiative's development and implementation. These leaders represented law enforcement, health care, education, business, the media, and other community sectors crucial to building a city-wide initiative. Next, this group worked with this father to plan, promote, and hold a city summit that attracted hundreds of other leaders to learn more about the initiative, help plan its overall strategy, and identify the sector-specific tactics for supporting father involvement. Finally, he identified a non-profit organization in the community that already supported fathers' involvement to lead the initiative and hold community leaders accountable for carrying out their parts of the overall plan.

This story provides an example of how just one father can have a broad impact on his community by helping many other fathers at once. In this father's case, he engaged his community to create an initiative designed to help fathers. But a father can engage his community in many other ways that indirectly support other fathers by improving specific aspects of the community in which he and other fathers live. To help you start identifying some ways in which you can engage your community and support fathers indirectly, complete the following statements:

- Three examples of a community's civic life are

  _____, _____, and _____.

- One way in which I'm engaged in my community is

  _____.

- One way I'm not engaged in my community but would like to be is

  _____.

The 24:7 Dad engages in his community's civic life. This engagement can take various forms, such as volunteering with an organization that serves a diverse population, joining or starting a ministry in your faith community focused on alleviating a specific problem like poverty or child abuse and neglect, contacting or working with elected officials to pass laws addressing issues you care about, or running for public office.

Civic engagement is beneficial for anyone. It offers psychological benefits similar to those of mentoring.[6] People engaged civically in their communities report better psychological and physical health. Civic engagement expands a person's overall social capital, including

---

[6]Sokolovsky, A. W., O'Neill, A. L., & Hope, E. C. (2024). Examining the relationship between civic engagement and mental health in young adults: A systematic review of the literature. *Journal of Applied Developmental Psychology, 91*, 101651.

social networks.[7] For men, it can reduce depression and the mental strain associated with unemployment.[8,9] It can also increase men's overall life satisfaction.[10] All you have to do is decide which form of engagement to use! The deep-dive activity at the end of this chapter will help you do that.

Quick Win: Starting a Fathering Support Group, Workshop, or Program

A great way to engage your community in a way specifically designed to support fathers is to start a fathering support group, workshop, or program. A support group creates a safe space for fathers to open up emotionally and support each other on an ongoing basis. Fathers may come and go, and the group's composition will likely change. To invite fathers to join the group, you can take one or both of the following approaches. Invite fathers in your circle of influence, whether

---

[7]Office of Disease Prevention and Health Promotion. (n.d.). *Civic participation*. Healthy People 2030. U.S. Department of Health and Human Services. https://odphp.health.gov/healthypeople/priority-areas/social-determinants-health/literature-summaries/civic-participation

[8]Yang, D. (2024). Impact of social participation on rural male population's mental health: Evidence from the 2020 China family panel studies. *Journal of Men's Health, 20*(11), 105–111.

[9]Wang, S., Ling, W., Lu, Z., Wei, Y., Li, M., & Gao, L. (2022, June 2). Can volunteering buffer the negative impacts of unemployment and economic inactivity on mental health? Longitudinal evidence from the United Kingdom. *International Journal of Environmental Research and Public Health, 19*(11), 6809.

[10]Sánchez-García, L., Díez, M., Sánchez-Queija, I., Lizaso, I., & Parra, Á. (2024). Civic engagement in emerging adulthood: Variation by gender and SES, and association with personal adjustment. *SAGE Open, 14*(4). https://doi.org/10.1177/21582440241293678

friends or acquaintances. This is a good approach to build experience in running a support group. Think of it as a hybrid form combining elements of paying it forward and engaging your community. It draws from the focus on your circle of influence in paying it forward and helping many fathers at once in engaging your community.

The other approach is to partner with an organization in your community to start a group for fathers you don't know. This approach involves working with an organization that serves families in some capacity that you think may welcome the opportunity. Examples include educational, health care, childcare, faith-based, and other non-profit and government organizations that offer programs or services, especially for parents. They can also include employers willing to provide a space for you to meet with fathers before, during (lunch time), or after work. If you want to start a support group, consider using this book as the resource. You can have fathers read portions of it for discussion at each meeting.

A workshop or program is like a support group in that it offers a safe space for fathers to open up emotionally and support each other. You can also promote a workshop or program to fathers within or outside your circle of influence, and to fathers you know or don't know. Where a workshop or program differs from a support group is the limited time a workshop or program lasts, which could be as little as one day (a workshop) or several months (a program). And while you can use this book as a resource to inform the content of a workshop or program, this approach is ideal for using an NFI workshop or program designed for this format that, like this book, draws from evidence about what works in helping fathers. These resources provide you with everything you need to run a workshop or program, including a manual for leading it and a workbook for the fathers. There's no guesswork. Plus, NFI can train you on how to implement the workshop or program and will provide help whenever you need it. Visit fatherhood.org to learn more about NFI's workshops and programs.

As you consider topics to explore in a support group, workshop, or program, I recommend including how fathers can raise resilient children. (Think of this guidance as a quick win within a quick win.) As children become more independent and learn to navigate life on their own, resilience will help them recover quickly from the difficulties they encounter. Share the following 10 experiences that research shows build resilience and encourage fathers to ensure their children have as many of these experiences as possible[11]:

- Unconditional love from caregivers
- Having a best friend
- Being part of a social group
- Having a mentor
- Volunteering
- Living in a safe and clean home with enough food
- Getting a good education
- Having a hobby
- Engaging in regular physical activity
- Having family routines and consistent rules

Take a moment to re-read that list. Think about which of the 10 experiences fathers can leverage immediately, regardless of their children's ages, and which they might need to build in when their children are older. (If a father has an infant, for example, he can wait to ensure his child has a mentor and a hobby!)

Give yourself a gold star if you identified unconditional love from caregivers, living in a safe and clean home with enough food, and

---

[11]Collins, A. M., & Johnson, S. I. (2021). Opportunities for psychologists to enact community change through adverse childhood experiences, trauma, and resilience networks. *American Psychologist, 76*(2), 379–390.

having family routines and consistent rules as the experiences fathers can leverage right away. Depending on their children's ages, fathers might also be able to help their children with the other seven experiences. Challenge fathers to plan for how they'll ensure their children have as many of the 10 experiences as possible.

Customizing the Habit

It's time to customize how you'll engage your community. This decision starts by reflecting on the following questions:

- How will I use what I've learned in this chapter about engaging my community?
- Do I prefer a direct or indirect approach in supporting many fathers at once?
- What are some ideas for engaging my community based on my preferred approach in supporting fathers?
- Looking at the ideas for engaging my community in the way I prefer, which one(s) do I choose?

When customizing this habit, using ways that involve interacting with your community is a given. You can combine that customization option with any of the other six options in Chapter 1. For example, you could volunteer in your community with your children, co-parent, friends, or co-workers.

Throughout this book, I've reminded you to consider habit stacking in deciding how to customize the habits, and I've provided some hypothetical examples of habit stacking. Here's an actual example of habit stacking that a father that I know used to engage his community in starting a fathers' support group. He focused on inviting fathers in his circle of influence by partnering with the elementary school one of his children attended. The school agreed to let him hold the group meetings on the third Saturday of every month. To invite fathers to join the group, he leveraged his habit of dropping off and picking up his child from school twice a week to establish a new habit of handing out flyers about the support group to other fathers dropping off and picking up (and to mothers to give to their children's fathers). He would either arrive a little early when dropping off or stay a little longer after picking up to hand out the flyers, and with the help of his child. This was not only a great use of habit stacking, but also a brilliant recruitment and retention tactic that constantly reminded fathers about the group who had never attended it and fathers who had attended to keep returning. Frequent communication is essential when promoting the availability of a fathers' support group, workshop, or program to ensure its success.

Deep-Dive Activity

The following activity will help you identify one or two ways in which you can engage your community.

Stewardship Skills: My Civic Engagement[12]

Identifying ways in which you can engage your community starts with assessing your willingness to contribute to your community by

---

[12] I drew on the following sources to create this activity: (1) Lee, S. (2025, May 24). *Civic engagement 101: A beginner's guide.* Number Analytics. https://www.numberanalytics.com/blog/civic-engagement-101; (2) Human Rights Careers. (n.d.). *How to become a community activist.* https://www.humanrightscareers.com/issues/how-to-become-a-community-activist/; (3) eScribe. (2025, April 16). *Citizen engagement: Enhancing your community engagement efforts.* https://www.escribemeetings.com/blog/improve-citizen-engagement/; and (4) Instant Input. (2023, July 1). *8 steps to create a community engagement plan.* https://www.instantinput.com/blog/community-engagement-plan

becoming civically active. Ask yourself, "How willing am I to engage my community in a meaningful way?" Use a scale of 0–5, with 0 = "not at all" and 5 = "completely." If you answered with a 4 or 5, you're ready to engage. Continue this exercise with the following steps. If you answered with a 0–3, wait to engage until you're more willing by gaining more experience as a 24:7 Dad who pays it forward one father at a time. Then, return to this exercise and see if you're ready to engage.

Step 1: Assess Your Ability and Capacity

If you're ready to become civically active, assess your ability to be helpful. Ask yourself, "What community issues concern me the most?" After you write those down, place a checkmark or star next to any of the issues you can help address using your knowledge, skills, or experience. Then, write down the specific knowledge, skills, or experience that will help address them.

Next, assess your capacity to dedicate the time necessary to help address the issue(s). Ask yourself, "How much time can I realistically dedicate to addressing the issue(s)?" To help you answer that question, consider asking anyone you know who might be engaged in addressing the issue(s) and can provide insight into the level of commitment that will make a difference. If you chose more than one issue, decide whether you have enough time to address all of them, keeping in mind that it's a good idea to plan for more time than you think may be required of you.

Step 2: Consider the Consequences

If you determine that you have the time for civic involvement, consider the potential second-order consequences (the mental model you learned about in Chapter 6). Specifically, assess the impact of this civic commitment on your family, work, *and yourself*. Ask yourself, "Will this commitment take time from my family and work commitments?"

and "How might this commitment affect me?" If it won't take time from family and work or affect you negatively, such as increasing your stress, that's great. However, if the commitment is likely to produce any of those outcomes, think twice about taking it on, while keeping in mind there may be ways to mitigate those outcomes. For example, if the commitment takes time from family, determine whether you can include them in addressing the issue(s). Perhaps they could volunteer with you. If the commitment takes time from work, determine whether you can frame this commitment so that your employer will support it. Perhaps your volunteering for a specific organization could shine a positive light on your employer. If the commitment has potential negative effects on you, however, the personal cost may be too steep.

Step 3: Test the Water

If the first two steps point to "yes," set a goal or objective for the level of impact you want to have. Then, create a plan that tests your assumptions about the level of commitment addressing the issue(s) will require. Pay attention to the actual consequences of this commitment on your family, work, and yourself. Include a date by which you'll evaluate the commitment and its consequences. Don't dive in headfirst. Put a toe in the water by starting with a small commitment and increasing from there until you find the right commitment for the level of impact you want. If you need to acquire knowledge or skills for this commitment, include that in the earliest stage of your plan.

Step 4: Evaluate

Determine whether to continue with the commitment as is, adjust it, or eliminate it. You can also decide whether to add another issue(s), such as the one you might have not chosen in the first step, or make a larger commitment to the current one(s).

AI Prompts

Here are two hypothetical prompts I created for paying it forward and engaging your community. These are only examples of how AI can be helpful in identifying ways to apply both habits.

- **Paying it forward.** I want to develop a list of three or four fathers who might be open to me mentoring them on fathering. I'll focus on fathers from my personal and professional networks. Advise me on identifying fathers most likely to be open to being mentored. Provide a sequence of steps for me to identify a good approach.

- **Engaging your community.** I'm a non-custodial father who has benefited from a fathering group and would like to start one for other non-custodial fathers. Acting as a community engagement specialist, help me recruit non-custodial fathers into a fathering support group. Because I have limited time to recruit fathers, provide me with your top five recruitment tactics.

The AI I used provided five steps to help me identify other fathers for mentoring. The steps began with defining my mentorship focus and style, such as the areas of fathering I'm most qualified to mentor on. The third step involved criteria to identify fathers who might be the most open to mentoring. The final step included sample scripts for inviting them.

For recruiting non-custodial fathers to join a support group, the AI recommended several tactics that I often recommend to NFI's partner organizations, including recruiting through organizations likely to serve non-custodial fathers, such as child support enforcement, family courts, and legal aid. It recommended crafting marketing messages that appeal to non-custodial fathers by focusing on what they'll gain from the group, such as help meeting basic needs and learning how to address challenges with child support. It also recommended creating a fun, casual event for fathers only, or fathers and their children, such as a cookout, and introducing the support group's availability during the event.

Chapter 8

Stepping Out of Your Comfort Zone

"In a growth mindset, challenges are exciting rather than threatening. So rather than thinking, oh, I'm going to reveal my weaknesses, you say, wow, here's a chance to grow."

—Carol Dweck, psychologist

In the movie *The Dark Knight Rises*, the last installment in the Batman trilogy starring Christian Bale, Bruce Wayne faces a commitment test. As Batman, he's nearly beaten to death by the villain Bane, who takes over Gotham City. After the beating, which leaves Wayne physically and emotionally broken, Bane sends him to a hidden prison in a foreign country that only one person has ever escaped from. Wayne faces a choice: he can give up and die, or re-dedicate himself to becoming an even better Batman. Of course, he chooses the latter. He first rebuilds his body to become stronger than before. Then he faces a life-threatening challenge that's essential for escaping the prison.

Escaping the prison requires a symbolic yet very real leap of faith. For an inmate to escape, he must climb the circular, slippery wall of an open hole that leads to the surface. If an inmate reaches a certain point on the wall, he must jump across the hole and grasp a small ledge on the other side to pull himself up. From there, it's a piece of cake. The standard method is to tie a rope around the waist so that if the inmate falls short during the jump, the rope will prevent a fall. Wayne tries the jump multiple times with the rope tied around his waist, but he fails each time. After a confidant in the prison challenges him to fully commit to the jump by not using the rope, he tries again and finally succeeds.

In 2018, I met a young man who reminded me of that version of Bruce Wayne. I was helping facilitate a strategic planning meeting for the Iowa Department of Human Services' (IDHS) effort to better engage non-custodial fathers who owe child support. Participants included IDHS staff and their local organization partners who served non-custodial dads. Many of those organizations used National Fatherhood Initiative® (NFI) programs. A representative of one organization was a father in his 20s. He was bright and offered many excellent suggestions for the strategic plan. I couldn't recall meeting someone his age who was more impressive.

I approached the executive director of the organization he represented to share how impressed I was and asked about his background. What I heard drove home how much change some fathers must go through just to be with their children. He was a recovering alcohol and drug addict. The state's child welfare program had removed his children from his and the mother's home. Soon thereafter, he went to rehab, but the mother refused treatment. While he was in rehab, he became a client of the organization he represented at the strategic planning meeting. He enrolled in an NFI program they offered. He did so well in it that the organization hired him to assist with running it. They soon promoted him to manage the entire program. While he was doing all that, he started visiting his children, whom the child welfare program had placed with relatives. He eventually gained full custody of them, raising them as a single father.

That young man reminded me to keep stepping out of my comfort zone. Writing this book required taking another step beyond it. I shared more of my past than I planned. My reward was that, by expanding the boundaries of my comfort zone, I healed my father wound even further. That wouldn't have happened if not for you and the other readers. Because of you, I was able to open up about some of my darkest times. Thank you for giving me that opportunity.

I encourage you to step outside your comfort zone as you develop the 12 habits of the 24:7 Dad. In his book *The Comfort Crisis: Embrace Discomfort to Reclaim Your Wild, Happy, Healthy Self*, men's health advocate and outdoorsman Michael Easter states, "Most people today rarely step outside their comfort zones. We are living progressively sheltered, sterile, temperature-controlled, overfed, underchallenged, safety-netted lives. And it's limiting the degree to which we experience our 'one wild and precious life', as poet Mary Oliver put it." While he mainly emphasizes the physical health benefits that wilderness experiences can offer, he makes an important point. Experiencing nature as our ancestors did is part of what makes us human. I can't think of anything that makes a man more human than raising the next generation. Men can choose not to do that, of course, since choice is also part of being human. However, when men become fathers, they owe it to their children to help them grow into successful adults. (They also owe it to their co-parent and every other person on this planet.)

The good news is that the fathering confidence you'll gain by developing the 12 habits will greatly influence your ability to help your children succeed both now and in the future. However, you need to build on what you've learned in this book. That may require stepping out of your comfort zone. Be intentional and proactive in learning what research and evidence tell us about what helps children become successful adults and parents. I'll leave you with three lessons that helped me step out of my comfort zone and made a major impact on my fathering: focusing on helping my children find their purpose in life, adopting a growth mindset, and raising awareness of my cognitive biases.

Purpose in Life

The first lesson is learning how to help your children develop autonomy, mastery, and purpose in ways that align with their interests. In Chapter 5, I explained how those forces form a three-legged stool that serves as the foundation of intrinsic motivation in anyone, including your children. I called that foundation Fathering's Long Game. When adults have all three elements in any part of their lives, it fuels motivation from within and helps them succeed both now and in the future. Autonomy fosters deep engagement, which is necessary for a full commitment to a purpose. Mastery means gaining the knowledge and skills needed to achieve that purpose.

I shared that insight as part of developing your ability to effectively discipline your children, which helps them build the autonomy needed to discover and pursue their purpose in life, as well as the desire to excel in fulfilling that purpose. What I didn't mention was that purpose is the most crucial of the three legs. Purpose supercharges autonomy and mastery by motivating people to make the most of their independence and skill so that they can excel rather than just get by. You can see the difference having purpose makes in comparing people with "a higher calling." These people have latched on to a belief, value, cause, or outcome that positively impacts others' lives. They also define success on their own terms.

Your role in helping your children find their purpose starts with helping them identify their interests by exposing them to lots of experiences. When they start showing an interest, your role shifts to helping them explore that interest by helping them develop autonomy and mastery to do it well, such as training on how to play a musical instrument for a child who shows interest in that instrument or buying a cookbook for a child who enjoys cooking and letting them prepare a meal. Children's interests can shift throughout childhood. But in helping them explore their interests and the importance of autonomy and mastery, you'll help lay the foundation for finishing construction of the three-legged stool at some point.

Growth Mindset

The second lesson builds on the first. Dr. Carol Dweck, a prominent psychologist, has done extensive research on how people view the nature of intelligence and other abilities as either a fixed or growth (changeable) mindset.[1] The fixed mindset is based on the belief that a person's intelligence, attitudes, beliefs, and abilities are static and can't be developed. The growth mindset, on the other hand, is based on the belief that these qualities can be improved and expanded. A person might have a fixed or growth mindset overall, or a combination where some traits are seen as fixed and others as adaptable. Whether someone generally has one mindset or the other explains many differences in how they behave and approach challenges. For example, when it comes to personal growth, a person with a fixed mindset tends to be very sensitive and dismissive when receiving suggested areas for improvement. Conversely, someone with a growth mindset usually remains open and receptive to such suggestions.

Children with a growth mindset handle major transitions better than those with fixed mindsets. For example, when moving from elementary to middle school, children with a growth mindset don't experience the drop in academic performance that children with a fixed mindset often do. In fact, they tend to perform even better. This period challenges children not only academically but also physically, as they enter puberty, and socially, as social groups form and children try to fit in. This advantage for growth-mindset children carries over to the

---

[1]Dweck, C. S. (2006). *Mindset: The new psychology of success*. Random House.

college transition, where they're more likely to take responsibility for their learning, primarily due to their intrinsic motivation.

The first step in cultivating a growth mindset in your children is to have one yourself. Children are more likely to develop a growth mindset when their parents have it. Parents with this mindset are more likely to offer their children the type of support that promotes hard work.[2,3] You probably have a growth mindset or are adopting it; otherwise, you wouldn't be reading this book. Nevertheless, if you want to determine which mindset you have, take the short quiz from *Psychology Today* at psychologytoday.com/us/tests/personality/growth-mindset-test.

Beyond modeling a growth mindset, cultivating it in your children involves consistently placing them in situations that challenge them to grow, praising them more for effort than outcomes, and reminding them that change and adapting to it are a normal part of life, as is accepting failure as a step in achieving their objectives. You should also encourage your children to self-reflect regularly, both solo (as with journaling) and with you and your co-parent (perhaps by asking them questions during shared meals). They should reflect on what they tried to do or accomplish, the level of difficulty, what they learned, and how they can grow and do better the next time if they didn't achieve their objective. Finally, identify activities that you can do with your children and co-parent that require everyone involved to learn something new. This collaborative or shared growth is a great way to create a family environment

---

[2] Song, Y., Barger, M. M., & Bub, K. L. (2022). The association between parents' growth mindset and children's persistence and academic skills. *Frontiers in Education, 6*, 791652.

[3] Rowe, M. L., & Leech, K. A. (2019). A parent intervention with a growth mindset approach improves children's early gesture and vocabulary development. *Developmental Science, 22*(4), e12792.

that fosters a growth mindset.[4,5,6] The psychology department at Stanford University offers a free online course for parents on cultivating a growth mindset in children. You can find it at https://www.mindsetkit.org/growth-mindset-parents. It takes only 30 minutes to complete.

Cognitive Biases

The third lesson was passed down to me by Dr. Wade Horn, a child psychologist and the first president of NFI. We were in his office late one afternoon discussing some of the dangerous behavior we engaged in during our childhoods and how we emerged unscathed. He said, "Don't project your outcomes onto your children. Just because you didn't have a bad outcome, Chris, don't assume your children will fare the same." That lesson motivated me to do everything I could to help my daughters avoid the numerous risky behaviors I had engaged in. They still engaged in their share, but likely far less than if not for that lesson.

Although I didn't realize it at the time, Wade helped me avoid falling into three cognitive biases that can trap even the best fathers.

---

[4]Tian, J., Bennett-Pierre, G., Tavassolie, N., Newcombe, N. S., Weinraub, M., Hindman, A. H., Newton, K. J., & Gunderson, E. A. (2023). A growth mindset message leads parents to choose more challenging learning activities. *Journal of Intelligence, 11*(10), 193.

[5]Gunderson, E. A., Gripshover, S. J., Romero, C., Dweck, C. S., Goldin-Meadow, S., & Levine, S. C. (2013). Parental praise to young children predicts motivational frameworks five years later. *Child Development, 84*(5), 1526–1541.

[6]Adamache, C. (2025, February 3). *Creating a growth mindset environment at home*. WMB Childcare Nurseries. https://wmbchildcare.co.uk/creating-a-growth-mindset-environment-at-home/

The first is the optimism bias, which involves overestimating the chance of a positive outcome and underestimating the chance of a negative one. The second is the false consensus effect, which involves overestimating how much others share your beliefs, attitudes, and behaviors. The third is the anecdotal fallacy, which involves taking one example and generalizing it to a larger group. This triple threat can cause a father to assume that because he successfully navigated a risky situation in his childhood that his children also face, his children will have the same outcome, just because they're his children. He may believe that the factors that helped him avoid a negative outcome—such as resilience or dumb luck—are also at play for his children. He concludes that his experience is typical of anyone engaging in the same behavior, including his children.

It's crucial to step back and objectively assess the risks when your children consider behavior that could harm them or others. If you engaged in the same or similar behavior, ask whether you're projecting your outcome onto your children. Also, ask whether you might be wrong in how you're assessing the risks. This could involve discussing the situation with your co-parent, accountability partner, or someone else you trust to provide honest feedback.

It won't be easy to step out of your comfort zone to become the confident father you want to be and your children need you to be. At this point, I could ask you to complete a statement or two that reveals you've probably stepped out of your comfort zone a few times and found success. But I won't do that. I'll leave you instead with the knowledge that you have the tools to become that confident father—a 24:7 Dad. It's time to knock fathering right out of the park!

Appendix

The Value in Married Fatherhood

If you're an unmarried father (or father-to-be) and questioning the *value* in being a married father, I have a crucial message for you: Being a married father is in your best interest and your children's best interest. Notice that I said the "value" and not the "desire." Someone can desire to be a married parent but question its value.

I've been where you are. Growing up with parents whose marriage should have ended long before it did, led me to question marriage's value. My parents divorced in my senior year of high school, at a time when the divorce rate in the United States was at its peak. Most of my closest friends were also children of divorce. We wondered whether being married was worth it and was in anyone's best interest.

Nevertheless, I wanted to be a married father—I desired it. Even now, I don't understand why I was so committed to raising children as a married father, especially since I didn't learn about the wealth of evidence supporting marriage's benefits until I joined National Fatherhood Initiative®. Maybe it was serendipity or divine intervention. Whatever the reason, I'm so glad I committed to being a married father.

Let me be clear about two things before continuing this discussion. First, any father, married or not, can become a 24:7 Dad. Second, any child, whether growing up with married parents or not, can have a wonderful childhood and become a happy, successful adult. This discussion isn't about an absolute—that you must be married to be a successful father and for your children to thrive. It's about how being married can enrich your fathering journey and how growing up with married parents can benefit your children now and in the future.

A Compelling Case

Let's start by explaining why being married is in your best interest. *It offers a better chance at leading a fulfilling life.* That fact might be hard to swallow, depending on your experience with marriage. If you're like most Americans, you don't see marriage as all that important. According to a nationally representative survey by the Pew Research Center on what makes life fulfilling, only 29 percent of men said that marriage is important.[1]

The negative perspective on marriage's role in a fulfilling life is contradicted by the evidence showing that married adults are more fulfilled than unmarried adults. The ongoing Global Flourishing Study investigates the factors that lead to adults flourishing, which means "a multidimensional state of well-being that involves positive emotions, engagement, relationships, meaning, and accomplishment." The study, involving over 200,000 adults across 22 countries and planned to be repeated every five years, assesses six areas of a flourishing life, including happiness, life satisfaction, and purpose, to assign a flourishing score to each participant. The first wave of the study revealed that married adults had a significantly higher average flourishing score compared to widowed, cohabiting, never married, divorced, and separated adults.[2]

---

[1] Horowitz, J. M., Graf, N., & Livingston, G. (2019, November 6). *Marriage and cohabitation in the U.S.* Pew Research Center. https://www.pewresearch.org/social-trends/2019/11/06/marriage-and-cohabitation-in-the-u-s/

[2] Counted, V., Johnson, B. R., & VanderWeele, T. J. (2025, May 1). *What makes people flourish? A new survey of more than 200,000 people across 22 countries looks for global patterns and local differences.* The Conversation. https://theconversation.com/what-makes-people-flourish-a-new-survey-of-more-than-200-000-people-across-22-countries-looks-for-global-patterns-and-local-differences-243671

An analysis of Census Bureau data shows that marriage's contribution to flourishing extends to parents, at least in the United States. Married parents are much happier than unmarried ones. This was true for both fathers and mothers. The percentage of males who reported being "very happy" was 35 percent for married fathers, 30 percent for married, childless men, 14 percent for unmarried, childless men, and 12 percent for unmarried fathers.[3] The percentage of married fathers was not only the highest among all males but also nearly three times that of unmarried fathers!

One reason married fathers are happier than other fathers and men is the benefits they gain from being married. Married men are healthier physically and mentally than unmarried men.[4] They're also better off financially.[5] Marriage also benefits men more than it benefits women, especially when married men are also fathers. Americans understand that. The Survey Center on American Life found that 58 percent of American men and 53 percent of American women agree that married fathers are happier than other men. In contrast, only 40 percent of men and 32 percent of women agree that married mothers are happier than other women.[6]

---

[3]Wilcox, B., & Wang, W. (2023, September 12). *Who is happiest? Married mothers and fathers, per the latest general social survey*. Institute for Family Studies. https://ifstudies.org/blog/who-is-happiest-married-mothers-and-fathers-per-the-latest-general-social-survey

[4]Robles, T. F., Slatcher, R. B., Trombello, J. M., & McGinn, M. M. (2014). Marital quality and health: A meta-analytic review. *Psychological Bulletin, 140*(1), 140–187.

[5]Zhang, Y. (2022). Marriage premium: A meta-analysis. *Journal of Economic Surveys, 36*(4), 1123–1147.

[6]Ekins, E. (2024, June 27). *Is marriage better for men?* American Survey Center. https://www.americansurveycenter.org/newsletter/is-marriage-better-for-men/

Let me be clear. Marriage isn't always in the best interest of every father's well-being. An unhealthy marriage can be toxic for you, your co-parent, and your children, especially when domestic violence or child abuse occurs. But if you're a never-married father, or about to become one, and unsure about getting married, the experiences of most married fathers should make you think twice. Even if you've been married and have a negative view of marriage, don't completely rule it out in the future.

An Even More Compelling Case

An even more compelling case for you being married is why it's in your children's best interest. *It provides them with a better chance at a fulfilling life.* Recent decades have seen a disconnect between marriage and parenthood, which is the most significant factor that leads to the separation of children from their fathers. When children grow up without their father, it places those children at greater risk for the negative outcomes you learned about in Chapter 1. Three trends have contributed to the separation of fathers and children: divorce, cohabitation, and out-of-wedlock births, with the last two being the main drivers today. (There's good news about marriage stability. A much larger percentage of couples who married in the 2010s were still married after 10 years than couples who married in any decade since the 1960s.)[7]

Cohabitation (living together) has become the normal pathway to marriage in the United States and an increasingly common pathway to parenting. Most married United States couples cohabitate

---

[7]Bailey, G., Stone, L., & Wilcox, B. (2024, July 24). *Divorce in decline: About 40% of today's marriages will end in divorce.* Institute for Family Studies. https://ifstudies.org/blog/divorce-in-decline-about-40-of-todays-marriages-will-end-in-divorce

before marriage.[8] Additionally, nearly half of all children are born to unmarried mothers, with half of those births to cohabiting couples.[9] Children born to cohabiting parents are much more likely than children born to married parents to see their parents split up, separating them most often from their fathers.[10]

Out-of-wedlock childbirths in the United States have skyrocketed. They represent 4 in 10 births, nearly double the rate in 1980.[11] When children are born to unmarried parents, they're much less likely to live with their father. Single mothers head nearly 8 in 10 single-parent households.[12]

The Impact on Your Children

Growing up with married parents has advantages for children that start with the obvious: their fathers are physically present. That doesn't mean their fathers are involved emotionally, intellectually, or

---

[8]Manning, W. D., & Carlson, L. (2021). *Trends in cohabitation prior to marriage*. Family profiles, FP-21-04. Bowling Green, OH: National Center for Family and Marriage Research.

[9]Martinez, G. M., & Daniels, K. (2023). Fertility of men and women aged 15–49 in the United States: National survey of family growth, 2015–2019. *National Health Statistics Report, 179* (January 10, 2023). Washington, D.C.: U.S. Centers for Disease Control and Prevention.

[10]Fagan, J. (2019). Broadening the scope of father-child attachment research to include the family context. *Attachment & Human Development, 22*(1), 139–142.

[11]Osterman, M. J. K., Hamilton, B. E., Martin, J. A., Driscoll, A. K., & Valenzuela, C. P. (2025, March 18). Births: Final data for 2023. *National Vital Statistics Reports, 74*(1). National Center for Health Statistics, Centers for Disease Control and Prevention.

[12]U.S. Census Bureau. (2022). *One-parent unmarried family groups with own children under 18, by marital status of the reference person: 2022*. Washington, D.C.: U.S. Census Bureau.

spiritually, but that holistic involvement is significantly easier when fathers live with their children. Unmarried fathers risk being less involved in their children's lives as their children get older, which places their children at greater risk of negative outcomes. For example, a study of 3,407 unmarried-parents families examined the fathers' involvement when their children were one, three, and five. The fathers' involvement decreased over time and led to increasing levels of behavioral problems in their children. The mothers also experienced more depression and parenting stress as the fathers became less involved.[13]

If you're separated from your children, or eventually separate from them, you may encounter the numerous systemic and personal barriers that contribute to other unmarried fathers being less involved over time. These barriers include challenging government policies that make it hard to establish paternity or custody; community-based systems that lack help for fathers, such as family service programs, legal aid, and health care. Many unmarried fathers lack the communication and self-advocacy skills that help them avoid or mitigate those barriers. They can also encounter the mother's gatekeeping behavior that limits or prevents access to their children.[14]

Growing up with a married father reduces the risk that children will experience the negative outcomes mentioned in Chapter 1. Married-couple households experience fewer hardships than households with other family structures. These hardships include problems

---

[13]Choi, J., Kim, M., & Kunz, G. (2018). Longitudinal relationships between unmarried fathers' involvement and their children's behavior problems: Using latent growth modeling. *Children and Youth Services Review, 91*, 424–430.

[14]Caines, M. C., Rebman, P., & Harrison, P. A. (2019). Barriers to unmarried father involvement during infancy: Qualitative study from professionals' perspectives. *Maternal and Child Health Journal, 23*(5), 641–647.

accessing or getting quality food, paying bills, poor housing, and living in noisy, littered, or unsafe neighborhoods. Single-parent households experience the most hardships. Two factors give married-couple households this advantage: income and wealth-building capacity. The presence of two parents gives families financial resources, such as insurance, savings, and investments, that help avoid or weather hardships.[15] Even in wealthy families, children who grow up with married parents tend to fare better financially. They're more likely to graduate from college, earn more, and remain wealthy. The advantages aren't only financial. Regardless of income, children with married parents are less likely to become depressed, anxious, and have behavioral problems.[16]

Your Children's Future

Hopefully, I've raised your awareness about why being a married father is in your and your children's best interest. I also want to raise your awareness about the value in your children being married one day. To start this part of the discussion, take a moment to write down your answers to the following questions:

- How important is it for your children, or future children, to be married one day?
- When they become parents, how important is it for them to be married?

---

[15]Iceland, J., & Cho, J. (2025). Household living arrangements and disparities in hardship. *Demographic Research, 52*(20), 589–634.

[16]Bailey, G., & Wang, W. (2025, April 17). *Family structure matters for rich kids, too*. Institute for Family Studies. https://ifstudies.org/blog/family-structure-matters-for-rich-kids-too

If you're like most parents today, you might not see marriage as important for your children. In fact, only 1 in 5 parents say it's important. Parents mostly prioritize their children becoming financially independent and having a job or career they enjoy, with nearly 9 in 10 parents feeling this way.[17] That view is interesting given that nearly all teenagers, 96 percent of boys and 95 percent of girls, expect to marry.[18]

Here lies a critical disconnect for parents who don't place importance on their children marrying. If these parents' children don't marry, it will be harder for their children to achieve financial independence as adults, especially if they're female or become parents. Married-couple households under age 35 have more than nine times the net worth of unmarried female householders and more than three times the net worth of unmarried male householders. That gap only increases with age.[19]

If you don't think it's important for your children to marry, think again. I'm not saying that you should focus on their future income or net worth as the main measure of happiness. I also don't want you to harass them about the need to marry. However, sending a clear message about the importance of marriage and *when to marry* has

---

[17]Minkin, R., & Horowitz, J. M. (2023, January 24). *Parenting in America today*. Pew Research Center. https://www.pewresearch.org/social-trends/2023/01/24/parenting-in-america-today/

[18]Graham, K., Guzzo, K. B., & Manning, W. D. (2022). *Teens' self-reported expectations and intentions for marriage, cohabitation, and childbearing* (Research Brief). Marriage Strengthening Research and Dissemination Center. https://www.childtrends.org/publications/teens-self-reported-expectations-and-intentions-for-marriage-cohabitation-and-childbearing

[19]Sullivan, B., Hays, D., & Bennett, N. (2023, June). *The wealth of households: 2021* (Current Population Reports, P70BR-183). Washington, D.C.: U.S. Census Bureau.

never been more important, especially with the emerging research on the "Success Sequence."

The Success Sequence

The Success Sequence consists of three steps: (1) graduate from high school; (2) work full time; and (3) get married before having children. An impressive 97 percent of Millennials who followed these steps avoided poverty as adults. This holds true even for the most disadvantaged young adults. By adhering to these steps, 94 percent of young adults from low-income backgrounds, including those from single-parent households, avoided poverty. Additionally, they moved into middle- or higher-income brackets at remarkable rates, including 84 percent who grew up without both parents.[20]

The good news about the Success Sequence extends beyond the young adults who follow it. About one-half of babies are born to parents who followed the Success Sequence. When those adults become parents, their children are less likely to live in a home that depends on welfare programs like Medicaid or charity. Success Sequence parents were much more likely to cover the birth costs with insurance or their own funds instead of using welfare. Following the sequence accounted for 4 of every 5 births paid for through non-welfare sources.[21]

Do everything you can to motivate your children to follow the Success Sequence. They'll benefit from it, and so will your grandchildren!

---

[20] Wang, W., & Wilcox, B. (2022). *The power of the success sequence for disadvantaged young adults*. Institute for Family Studies. https://ifstudies.org/ifs-admin/resources/reports/successsequencedisadvantagedya-final.pdf

[21] Zill, N. (2025, June 4). *To reduce welfare dependence, America needs more 'success sequence' babies*. Institute for Family Studies. https://ifstudies.org/blog/to-reduce-welfare-dependence-america-needs-more-success-sequence-babies

Acknowledgments

This book wouldn't have been possible without the support of current and past National Fatherhood Initiative® (NFI) staff and board members. These individuals have contributed in various ways to helping me create and improve NFI's fathering programs and other resources. They've given me the freedom to experiment with NFI's resources and lent their expertise in developing those resources and training NFI's partner organizations in how to use them.

I also want to acknowledge the NFI's partner organizations and the fathers using NFI resources for serving as the proving ground for testing and refining what helps fathers the most in being the fathers they want to be and their children need them to be.

I want to thank the researchers whose studies on family strengthening, parenting, fathering, and behavior change provided the research-backed foundation for this book and the content of NFI's programs and resources. Without their work, I couldn't do what I love and matters most to me professionally: using research to create effective, practical tools that improve the human experience.

I want to thank the team of editors at Wiley who educated, challenged, and assisted me through the many months it took to move this book from start to finish. Thanks to Sam for approaching me to write this book and educating me about book publishing and marketing. Thanks to Melanie for improving the book's flow and coherence, making it more concise, and challenging me to include much more of myself—my words and experiences—in communicating the book's guidance. Her pinpoint thinking helped me produce a much better tool for fathers. Thanks to Sarah for applying the final grammatical and formatting touches. Thanks to Navin for answering numerous technical questions as I put the book together.

Most of all, I want to acknowledge the unwavering love of my wife, Kayla, and daughters, Alexis and Jillian, and the grace they've given me to be imperfect. I drew from their love and grace to accept that I could write an imperfect book that could still have the positive impact on fathers, mothers, children, and families that I've always strived for.

About the Author

Christopher A. Brown is the President of National Fatherhood Initiative®, the nation's leading organization equipping communities to strengthen the vital bond between fathers and their children. An anthropologist, husband, father, and grandfather, Christopher brings more than three decades of experience helping transform the lives of fathers, mothers, and families across the United States and beyond.

A nationally recognized leader in the fatherhood field, Christopher designed the country's most widely used evidence-based and research-informed fathering programs and has trained thousands of professionals serving fathers in every state. His insights have guided federal and state fatherhood initiatives, and he has been a trusted advisor on multiple national policy committees.

Christopher's work and commentary have been featured in major media outlets, including *The New York Times*, *Los Angeles Times*, *CNN*, and *Fox News*, and his influence extends globally—consulting with organizations on six continents to help launch and strengthen fatherhood initiatives worldwide. He lives in Cedar Park, Texas.

Index

Numerics
6 traits of 24:7 Dad
    fathering skills, 2, 68–69, 97
        holistic fathering, 69–80
        modeling healthy
            masculinity, 81–96
    parenting skills, 2, 101–102
        disciplining your children in
            healthy ways, 118–132, 135
        nurturing your children, 102–117,
            134–135
        self-worth survey, 132–134
    relationship skills, 2–3, 172–173
        communicating effectively,
            141–156, 173–174
        creating a loving co-parenting
            relationship, 156–171, 174
    self-awareness, 1–2, 5, 17
        in behavior change, 17
        core values, 29–30
        goal setting, 18
        intrinsic motivation, 18
        weekly reflection on your
            actions, 25–29
        working with an accountability
            partner, 19–24
    self-care, 2, 34–35
        messages from your child,
            63–64
        regular mental health, 43–63
        regular physical care, 35–43
    stewardship, 2–3, 5, 193–195
        engaging your community,
            186–193, 196
        paying it forward, 178–186, 196
12 habits of 24:7 Dad, 4. *See also specific individual traits*
    applying and customizing, 11–12
    communicating effectively, 141–156, 173–174
    creating a loving co-parenting
        relationship, 156–171, 174
    disciplining your children in healthy
        ways, 118–132, 135
    engaging your community,
        186–193, 196
    holistic fathering, 69–80
    modeling healthy masculinity, 81–96
    nurturing your children, 102–117,
        134–135
    paying it forward, 178–186, 196
    regular mental health, 43–63
    regular physical care, 35–43
    weekly reflection on your actions,
        25–29
    working with an accountability
        partner, 19–24
24:7 Dad. *See also specific entries*
    artificial intelligence (AI)
        tools, xxv, 30
    definition of, 1
    traits and habits, xxv

A

accountability partnership
  addressing mental health challenges, 20
  benefits, 19–21
  contributing factors
    clear objectives, 22
    complementary skills and perspectives, 21
    constructive feedback, 22
    mutual buy-in, 21
    regular meetings, 22
    trusting and safe environment, 22
  customizing the habit, 22–23
  improvements in physical activity, 20
  meeting with partner, 23–24
active listening, 148–150, 168, 170, 171
active participation in learning, xxiv
anxiety, xiv, 39, 50, 51, 92
artificial intelligence (AI) tools, xxv
  role recipe, 30
  steps recipe, 30
authoritarian parenting, 122, 158, 159
autonomy, 128–129, 202

B

blame and shame, 125
body image development with children, 92–95
body language, 152–155
  defensive/closed posture, 153–154
  fight/flight posture, 153
  open for change posture, 154, 155
boldness regret, 111

C

child development knowledge, 106–109
  online sources, 109
children without fathers, xxiii, 210
civic engagement, 188–189, 193–195
cognitive biases, 205–206
  anecdotal fallacy, 206
  false consensus effect, 206
  optimism bias, 206
cohabitation, 163, 210–211
comfort zone, expansion, 200–201
  adopting growth mindset, 203–205
  helping children to find purpose in life, 202–203
  raising awareness of cognitive biases, 205–206
commitment pledge, xxvi–xxvii
confidence, xvii, 82. *See also* fathering confidence
  lack of, xiii
confidentfathers.com, xxvii, 6
corporal punishment, 99, 124–125
cross-cultural masculinity traits, 84
  achieving success, 83
  ambition, 82
  assertiveness, 82
  being honorable, 83
  being respectful, 83
  competitiveness, 82
  confidence, 82
  courage, 82
  emotional control, 83
  emotional expressiveness, 85
  empathy, 85
  exerting power, 83
  nurturing, 85
  taking risks, 83
  vulnerability, 85

D

depression, xxi, 39, 45, 47–51, 63, 92, 93, 129, 144, 189, 212
developmental milestones, 107–109
The dictator style, 121
digital technology
  children's screen time, concerns, 115
  to promote children development
    educational shows and apps prioritization, 116
    examine your motives, 115
    face-to-face interactions prioritization, 116
    match screen time to your children's age, 116
    no screen time close to bedtime, 116

physical activity prioritization, 116
use digital technology together, 116
use privacy and parental controls, 116
discipline style
definition of, 120
The dictator, 121
The dreamer, 122
The follower, 121–122
The joker, 121
The king, 121–123, 125
reflective statements, 120
disciplining your children in healthy ways
customizing the habit, 131–132
discipline style, 120–123
Fathering's Long Game, 128–131
physical force, avoidance, 124–125
positive reinforcement, 127–128
positive reminders, 131
reflective reinforcement, 125–127
reflective statements, 118
role modeling, 119, 120
teaching morals and values, 119
walk the talk, 119
The dreamer style, 122

E

effective communication
active listening, 148–150
approaching conflict, 144–146
avoiding confrontation, 138
barriers, 141–142
body language, 152–155
customizing the habit, 156
finding compromise, 147–148
five-second rule, 155–156
Listening Filter™, 150–152
reflective statements, 142
resolving conflict, 142–144, 146–147
solution-focused language, 143
effective co-parenting, 76–77
foundation checklist, 77–78
emotional intimacy, 86–89, 92
empathy, 104, 162–166, 170, 171
extrinsic motivation, 74

F

father–child bonding, 104–106
father figures, xii, xiv, xvii, 70
fathering confidence, 18, 159, 201
continuity, xix–xx
definition, xviii
making resilient, xix
self-reinforcing cycle, xix
winning streaks, xix–xx
fathering losses, xix
fathering skills, 2, 97
holistic fathering
cultural environment, 71
customizing the habit, 80
economic changes, 73
effective co-parenting, 76–78
extrinsic motivation, 74
fathers' natural strengths, 74–76
gender-based division of responsibilities, 72
intrinsic motivation, 74
reflective statements, 70–71
relational factor, 69–71
time spent with their children, 72–73
using humor, 79
modeling healthy masculinity
cross-cultural masculinity traits, 82–85
customizing the habit, 95–96
discussing body image with children, 92–95
influential models, 81–82
intimacy, 85–89
sexuality, 89–92
Fathering's Long Game, 128–131, 202
focusing on a child's motivator, 129–130
focusing on what a child learned, 130
teaching child positive self-talk, 130
father's evolving role, 71–74
fathers' natural strengths, 74–76

father wound, xv, 45, 46, 138, 201
The follower style, 121–122

G
gender-based division of responsibilities, 72
grief
  crying, 53
  healthy ways to, 53
  stages of, 52
  through rituals, 52
growth mindset, 203–205

H
habit stacking, 9–10, 27
harsh-style parents, 122–123
healthy masculinity modeling
  cross-cultural masculinity traits, 82–85
  customizing the habit, 95–96
  discussing body image with children, 92–95
  influential models, 81–82
  intimacy, 85–89
  sexuality, 89–90
  sexual self-worth survey, 91–92
high-conflict co-parenting, 159
holistic fathering
  cultural environment, 71
  customizing the habit, 80
  economic changes, 73
  effective co-parenting, 76–78
  extrinsic motivation, 74
  fathers' natural strengths, 74–76
  gender-based division of responsibilities, 72
  intrinsic motivation, 74
  reflective statements, 70–71
  relational factor, 69–71
  time spent with their children, 72–73
  using humor, 79
humor, 79

I
interlocking contact, 75
intimacy
  abandoning families, 88
  communication skills, 88
  definition of, 86
  emotional intimacy, devaluing, 86, 87
  emotional intimacy with other men, 88–89
  pain point, 86
  physical intimacy, valuing, 86
  problems in romantic relationships, 87
intrinsic motivation, 18, 74, 128, 129, 157
  autonomy, 128–129, 202
  purpose, 128, 129, 202
involved fathers, benefits of, xx–xxi

J
The joker style, 121
journaling, 26–28, 64, 65

K
keystone habits, 8–9
The king style, 121–123, 125

L
Listening Filter™, 150–152
  criticizing, 150, 151
  giving advice, 150, 151
  talking about yourself, 150, 151
living vicariously, 109–112
losing streaks, xx
loving co-parenting relationship
  customizing the habit, 170–171
  empathy, 162–163
    muscle activation, 164–166
  I statement, 169–170
  parenting styles, 158–161
  positive child-rearing behaviors, 163–164
  power and control, 166–168
  reflective statements, 157–158
  signs of, 168

M

married fatherhood, value in
  children's future, 213–215
  cohabitation, 210–211
  flourishing life, 208, 209
  impact on your children, 211–213
  marriage benefits, 209
  Success Sequence, 215
mental health care
  action and commitment therapy, 46
  anger, 45
  customizing the habit, 62–63
  depression, 45, 47–51
  grief, 52–54
  loss, 51–52
  reflective statements, 44
  seeking help, 44
  stress/stressors, 47–48
  suggestions
    be content, 61
    be grateful, 60
    be patient, 61
    eliminate clutter, 61
    find a hobby, 61
    get enough sleep, 61
    get real, 61
    spend time with friends, 61
    volunteer, 61
  suppressing emotions, 46, 47
  work–family balance, 54–60
mentoring, 179–180, 182
  proactive mentoring, 183–184
  return on investment (ROI), 184–185
meta-analysis, 10
mother–child attachment, 105–106
mothers with engaged fathers, xxi
mutual touching, 75

N

National Fatherhood Initiative® (NFI)
  program, xix, 3, 17, 34, 45,
  74, 89, 109, 137, 142, 154,
  157, 162, 163, 175, 176,
  190, 200, 207
natural strengths of father, 74–76

non-custodial fathers, 200
nurturing your children
  building positive self-worth, 103
  customizing the habit, 117
  emotional foundation
    development, 105, 106
  empathy, 104
  establishing reading habit, 112–114
  hormonal changes, 104–105
  pain points to avoid
    lack of child development
      knowledge, 106–109
    living vicariously through your
      children, 109–112
  realistic goals, 103
  reflective statements, 103
  using digital technology, 114–117

O

online sources, child development
  knowledge, 109
out-of-wedlock childbirths, 211

P

parenting skills, 2
  disciplining your children in
    healthy ways
    customizing the habit, 131–132
    discipline style, 120–123
    Fathering's Long Game, 128–131
    physical force,
      avoidance, 124–125
    positive reinforcement, 127–128
    positive reminders, 131
    reflective reinforcement,
      125–127
    reflective statements, 118
    role modeling, 119, 120
    teaching morals and values, 119
    walk the talk, 119
    non-violent tactics, 101
  nurturing your children
    avoiding pain points, 106–112
    building positive self-worth, 103
    customizing the habit, 117

parenting skills (*continued*)
    emotional foundation
        development, 105, 106
    empathy, 104
    establishing reading habit, 112–114
    hormonal changes, 104–105
    realistic goals, 103
    reflective statements, 103
    using digital technology,
        114–117
    self-worth survey, 132–134
parenting styles, 158–160
    authoritarian parenting, 122, 158, 159
    differences in, 159–161
    high-conflict co-parenting, 159
paternal depression, 49, 50
paying it forward
    customizing the habit, 186
    definition of, 178
    mentoring relationship with other
        fathers, 179–180, 182
    minding age gap, 185
    proactive mentoring, 183–184
    reflective statements, 179
    by role modeling, 180–181
    sharing lesson, 178, 181
physical health care
    benefits for children, 39–40
    cardiovascular health, 39
    customizing the habit, 42–43
    declining physical activity, 38
    ignoring warning signs, 36
    physical activities with children
        assessing child's physical
            abilities, 40
        assessing your physical
            abilities, 40
        considering access to
            your child, 41
        creating a schedule, 41
        expand and change, 41
        experiment, observe, and
            adjust, 41
        identifying activities, 41
        identifying the resources at your
            disposal, 40

    reducing harmful behaviors, 38
    reflective statements, 36
    staying physically active, 37–40
    supporting your co-parent, 42
    weight gain, 38
physical intimacy, 86–88
pledge of commitment, xxvi–xxvii
positive reinforcement, 127–128
    freedoms, 128
    praise, 128
    presents, 128
    touch, 128
positive reminders, 131
punishment, 99, 118–120, 123, 124,
    126, 127, 135

Q

quick win
    accountability partnerships, 21–22
    age gap, 185
    children's body image, 92–95
    empathy, 164–166
    Five-Second Rule, 155–156
    I Statement, 169–170
    journaling, 26–28
    loving co-parenting relationship,
        168–169
    mental health, 60–62
    physically active with
        children, 40–42
    positive reminders, 131
    reading to children, 112–114
    starting a support group, 189–192
    using digital technology, 114–117
    using humor, 79
    ways to grieve, 53–54
    work–family balance, 57–60

R

reading habit, 112–114
    suggestions for, 113–114
reflective habit
    customizing the habit, 28–29
    journaling, 26–28
    questions, 26
    statements, 25

reflective reinforcement tactics, 125–127
  apologizing, 126
  express disappointment, 126
  grounding, 126
  removing freedom, 126
  time-out, 126
relational factors, fathering confidence, xviii, 69–71
relationship skills, 2–3, 172–173
  communicating effectively
    active listening, 148–150
    approaching conflict, 144–146
    avoiding confrontation, 138
    barriers, 141–142
    body language, 152–155
    customizing the habit, 156
    finding compromise, 147–148
    five-second rule, 155–156
    Listening Filter™, 150–152
    reflective statements, 142
    resolving conflict, 142–144, 146–147
    solution-focused language, 143
  creating a loving co-parenting relationship
    customizing the habit, 170–171
    empathy, 162–163
    empathy muscle activation, 164–166
    I statement, 169–170
    parenting styles, 158–161
    positive child-rearing behaviors, 163–164
    power and control, 166–168
    reflective statements, 157–158
    signs of, 168
  mental models, 140–141
  solvable differences, 172–173
role modeling, 119, 120, 180–181

S

self-awareness, 1–2, 5, 17
  in behavior change, 17
  core values, 29–30
  goal setting, 18
  intrinsic motivation, 18

weekly reflection on your actions
  customizing the habit, 28–29
  journaling, 26–28
  questions, 26
  reflective statements, 25
working with an accountability partner
  addressing mental health challenges, 20
  benefits, 19–21
  contributing factors, successful partnership, 21–22
  customizing the habit, 22–23
  improvements in physical activity, 20
  meeting with partner, 23–24
  reflective statements, 19
self-care, 2, 34–35
  messages from your child, 63–64
  regular mental health care
    action and commitment therapy, 46
    anger, 45
    customizing the habit, 62–63
    depression, 45, 47–51
    grief, 52–53
    loss, 51–52
    reflective statements, 44
    seeking help, 44
    stress/stressors, 47–48
    suggestions for, 60–61
    suppressing emotions, 46, 47
    work–family balance, 54–60
  regular physical care
    benefits for children, 39–40
    cardiovascular health, 39
    customizing the habit, 42–43
    declining physical activity, 38
    ignoring warning signs, 36
    physical activities with children, 40–41
    reducing harmful behaviors, 38
    reflective statements, 36
    staying physically active, 37–40
    supporting your co-parent, 42
    weight gain, 38

sexuality, 89–92. *See also* intimacy
sexual self-worth, 90
    survey, 91–92
social fathers, xvii
state of men's health, 37
stewardship, 2–3, 5, 193–195
    alumni programs, 176, 177
    assessing your ability and capacity, 194
    considering the consequences, 194–195
    engaging your community, 186–193, 196
        civic engagement, 188–189
        customizing the habit, 192–193
        fathering support group/workshop/program, 189–192
        reflective statements, 188
    evaluation, 195
    paying it forward
        customizing the habit, 186
        definition of, 178
        mentoring relationship with other fathers, 179–180, 182
        minding age gap, 185
        proactive mentoring, 183–184
        reflective statements, 179
        by role modeling, 180–181
        sharing lesson, 178, 181
    testing the water, 195
sympathetic pregnancy, 104

T
teenage depression, 50
transformative power of habits, 6–7
    cues, 8, 9, 28
    habits in autopilot mode, 8
    habit stacking, 9–10, 27
    keystone habits, 8–9
    reward, 8, 28
    routine, 8, 28

U
unmarried fathers, 207, 209, 212

W
walk the talk, 119
winning streaks, xix–xx
work–family balance, xxii, 85, 181, 182
    family side suggestions
        discussing about commitments, 59–60
        family contract, create and sign, 59
        limiting work on weekends, vacations, and holidays, 58
        make career decisions, 58
        spending time with family every day, 58–59
        turning off your mobile phone and laptop during family time, 59
        use shared family calendar, 59
    relationship with work, 55
    self-assessment questions, 56
    unpaid paternity leave, 54, 55
    value for work and family, 56
    work schedules, 54
    work side suggestions
        be a team player, 57
        be thoughtful about special jobs, 57
        informing co-workers about your family commitments, 57
        maintaining family and work commitment, 58
        making your boss an ally, 57
        show/share your children's artwork and family photos, 57–58
        staying busy and focused, 57
        use work benefits, 58